ECHOES OF SUCCESS

Modern Business – Marketing Methods & Salesmanship
Timeless Sales Lessons from 1914 – Volume 1

Written by
David C. Moravec

With Excerpts from
Butler, DeBower, Jones
Marketing Methods and Salesmanship

MODERN
BUSINESS

Marketing Methods and Salesmanship

PART I: MARKETING METHODS

BY

RALPH STARR BUTLER

ASSOCIATE PROFESSOR OF BUSINESS ADMINIS-
TRATION IN THE UNIVERSITY OF WISCONSIN

PART II: SELLING

PART III: SALES MANAGEMENT

BY

HERBERT F. DeBOWER

VICE PRESIDENT, ALEXANDER HAMILTON INSTITUTE

AND

JOHN G. JONES

SALES MANAGER, ALEXANDER HAMILTON INSTITUTE;
LECTURER ON SALESMANSHIP IN NEW YORK UNIVER-
SITY SCHOOL OF COMMERCE, ACCOUNTS AND FINANCE

Modern Business
Volume III

ALEXANDER HAMILTON INSTITUTE
NEW YORK

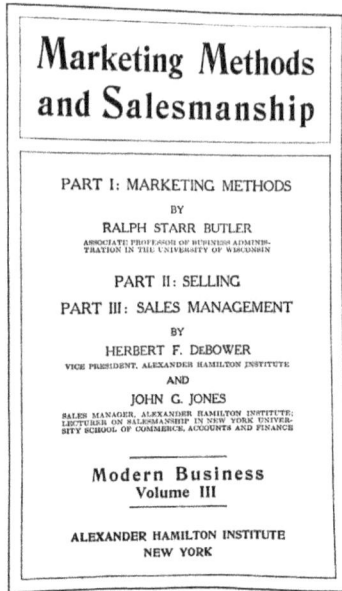

The original copyright for the material contained in this compilation was 1914. It is currently in the public domain of the United States and possibly other countries. As such, it is reproduced for historical purposes and to bring lessons from over 100 years ago into our 21st century.

Echoes of Success
Modern Business – Marketing Methods & Salesmanship
Timeless Sales Lessons from 1914 – Volume 1
Copyright ©2025 David C. Moravec

ISBN 978-1506-915-08-1 PBK
ISBN 978-1506-915-09-8 EBK

May 2025

Published and Distributed by
First Edition Design Publishing, Inc.
P.O. Box 17646, Sarasota, FL 34276-3217
www.firsteditiondesignpublishing.com

This book is dedicated to the many professionals who poured their lives into creating the works associated with the Modern Business series of books and the Alexander Hamilton Institute.

It is also dedicated to the 100's of thousands, if not millions, of people who benefited from the words, lessons, and methodology provided to business professionals across the globe who picked up the work or invested $150 to further their education formally.

ACKNOWLEDGEMENTS

The work contained in these pages is eleven years in the making. I am thankful for the cover design and brand recognition provided by Anna Sophia Beetge from South Africa. We initially collaborated on *Echoes Across the Tracks* and, most recently, with its companion sequel, Echoes to Remember. Anna is talented beyond her years and provides both professionalism and practicality from a design perspective.

Mentorship, leadership, and subject matter expertise come with time and success. Countless sales leaders have shaped my life over the years, far too many to mention. However, certain individuals make a mark that is indelible and foundational to one's character. Harlan and Chad Geiser, father and son who have integrity in every walk of life, come to mind first; both are true inspirations for me. Pat Helmers (of Sales Babble fame) helped shape me in a way others could not. Bob Burg, Jeff West, John Jantsch, Zig Ziglar, Tom Hopkins, Brian Tracy, and Pat Williams all played a part in shaping my sales leadership through their words of wisdom shared in countless pages of books lining my bookshelves. I hope their books and others adorn your bookshelves, not just for decoration, but as continuing education.

If you are a successful salesperson reading this today, you know what I mean. You know who influenced and encouraged you to stay the course when times got tough; am I right? You know who made you practice that presentation one more time, asked for call reports or CRM updates to be accurate, and worked alongside you to help mold you into the salesperson you are today. Who taught you the proper way to close and button up an order? Like many, you may have learned it on your own with countless failures along the way, but in the end, perseverance won out. Think about that as you read the pages ahead, because those who put the words on paper in 1914 can come alive for you today, if you just listen for the echoes to go through.

Echoes is thematic for me because of the repetition and consistency of those reverberating sounds. When you yell HELLO in a tunnel, the same word comes back to you, but it fades into the distance. The softer tone continues to resonate long after the original sound has passed. So true is it with sales lessons. Charlie is that guy in my head, the one who echoes a thought, an idea, a challenge, or a solution. Charlie (Charles) is my middle name and the main character in my inspirational parables, ***Echoes Across the Tracks*** and ***Echoes to Remember,*** and I decided to use him as the narrator of the words contained here. Make no mistake, Charlie is Dave, and Dave is Charlie. If you have a thought to share with either of us, please be sure to write or call.

Contents

Compilation & Author's Instructions

WHO - Who are you? I am not the author of the text you are about to read. The text was authored by R.S. Butler, Herbert F. DeBower, and John G. Jones on behalf of the Alexander Hamilton Institute in New York. However, I have added value to the text by providing professional insights and points to ponder, which I hope will draw you closer to the topic of Sales and Marketing. You might consider the background of the three men instrumental in putting this compilation together as you read.

- **Ralph Starr Butler** (1882-1971)-Ralph was born in Chicago and graduated from the University of Michigan at Ann Arbor. He was a lifelong thought leader in sales and marketing, joining forces with DeBower and Jones in collaboration on this and many other works at the Alexander Hamilton Institute. Ralph was an academic at his core but enjoyed an extensive business career. He was eventually inducted into the National Advertising Hall of Fame and retired as VP for General Foods in the 1950s.

- **Herbert F. Debower** (1873-1940) – Born in Dane County, Wisconsin, to earlier pioneer parents, he attended school and eventually became a professor at the University of Wisconsin at Madison. He practiced law for some time and founded the Alexander Hamilton Institute in 1909. He was active at the Institute until he died in 1940.

- **John G. Jones** (1869-1956) – Born in Wales, John attended the University College of Wales. Immigrating to the United States, he worked his way west working in the mining industry near Great Falls, MT. He served the Great Falls Chamber of Commerce from 1888 to 1897 before moving back to New York, where he helped start the Alexander Hamilton Institute with DeBower and others. John was president of the New York Sales Manager Club in 1932-1933 during the Depression era.

WHAT - What is it that I will be reading? The Alexander Hamilton Institute was an authoritative training organization based in New York and England. With various workshops, volumes of training materials, and business lessons, the institute created the Marketing & Salesmanship book you will be reviewing. It is now in the public domain, along with many other volumes with far-reaching business topics; it contains material no longer held to copyright standards. While I will assert that there is original material contained in this printed and e-book, written by me, the compilation intends to provide insights that are both universal to the sales profession and stand the test of time.

Modern Business: Marketing Methods and Salesmanship Volume III is a 586-page combination of encyclopedia and practical lessons on two essential topics: Marketing and Sales.

What struck me when I picked it up 10 years ago in 2014 was that the title included the word "Modern," and yet it was written in 1914!

WHEN - When did this come about? This book was originally copyrighted in 1914 and 1916. The series was revised, sometimes annually, until the 1980s when the organization was dissolved. As changes took place over the years, so did the technology, available resources, and business methods. The brainchild for bringing this together came in iterative forms for me over the last 10 years. As shared earlier, the Alexander Institute was founded in 1909 and dissolved as an organization in the mid-1980s.

WHERE - Where can I look at this book and your presentation? My answer is simple: right here and right now! With the technology available, you can read this material on your smartphone, Kindle, eReader, laptop, or in print form. You can take advantage of these lessons and apply them to your business or profession. But the more difficult question is, "Will you?" Will you share them with others?

WHY - Why have you created this piece of work? When I picked up the original book (leather bound) in 2014 at the Books to Benefit event in Normal, IL, there was no way to know how impactful it would be for me and others I've challenged over the last ten years. From the first reading, I recognized that this book held historical significance and personal appeal. In some ways, it reads like a King James Bible with lessons and prose from a different time period because it was. However, if we inserted the proper terminology from today and cross-referenced examples that are more applicable to today, we would essentially have the same work.

Today, business professionals, including me, have taught the importance of bringing marketing and sales into congruence. Congruence, by definition, includes agreement or harmony.

HOW - How did this all come together? Having wrestled with how best to convey my ideas in book form, I have provided an abridged version of the original text (approximately 5%), which can be purchased or accessed online through various methods. It has been preserved in scanned form to preserve the words for future generations. However, I contend that our society, which continues looking for a condensed response, will appreciate the lessons and text provided within these pages.

For additional training and a personalized approach, visit www.SalesManagerForRent.com.

Points to Ponder—Can you think of a time and place when Marketing and Sales were not harmonious? I think my list is enormous. The Alexander Hamilton Institute separated the two topics in later years and created distinct volumes for each. This action was not limited to marketing and sales but also those in operations and accounting, among others. Metaphorically and practically, having a sound marketing plan alongside your organization's sales philosophy and strategy is crucial.

The original book is broken up into three Parts:

    Part I – Marketing
    Part II – Selling
    Part III – Sales Management

Within each Part, there are Chapters and then topical numbers. Since I'm not presenting the information in order (front to back), I will reference the proper chapter and section.

Telephone and Automobile

Telephones Then and Today

At the start of World War I, in 1914, there were ten people for every working telephone in the U.S. By the end of World War II, in 1945, there were five people for every working phone. The technology passed a key milestone in 1998, when there was one phone for every man, woman, and child in the U.S.

Additionally, making a coast-to-coast phone call a century ago was very expensive. In 1915, a three-minute daytime phone call from New York City to San Francisco cost $20.70. Adjusted for inflation means the relatively brief call would cost more than

$500 in today's currency. Over the next half-century, prices fell drastically, although they were still pricey. In 1968, the same three-minute call cost $1.70 – or about $12 in today's currency. The time of day you called also had a different price structure. That's why personal calls were often made at night or over the weekend during off-peak times. While phone calls were much cheaper during those off-peak times, it was not practical from a business perspective, given the typical 9am-5pm workday.

Cell phone technology has dramatically advanced business concerns, even over my 40-year career. I recall two incidents that are worthy of sharing. In 1984, payphones cropped up in gas stations across Chicagoland and were placed on outdoor poles rather than just in phone booths. This allowed me to pull up to a phone in a gas station parking lot, roll down my window, and have a conversation in the privacy of my car; that was provided the cord itself was long enough to reach. If I stopped at the Mobil gas station, you might say that I had a "mobile phone."

Additionally, in 1990, a sales opportunity presented itself that was time sensitive. To make the sale happen, I needed access to a phone. I was in a rural part of NW Illinois at the time, and thankfully, my "bag-phone" cord reached from the cigarette lighter to the roof of my car. While standing on the running boards and stretching as far as I could, I gained a signal from a distant tower. Without that maneuver, it would have been a "stretch" for me to make the sale to this demanding customer.

Points to Ponder:

As you read these lessons, please consider how the telephone has changed your life over your lifetime, and consider how this device (landline) affected business in 1914 compared to today. Where will the internet, telecommunications, and artificial intelligence be in 5-10-20 years, let alone 100 years from now?

Planes, trains, and automobiles then and today

First built in 1893, gas engine vehicles were costly for a long time. By 1900, at least 100 different brands of "horseless carriages" were being marketed in the United States. Since they were all virtually handmade, the cars were outrageously expensive. Cars were perceived as no more than high-priced toys for the rich. In the early 1900s, cars were, to many people, a despicable symbol of arrogance and power. Nevertheless, people began buying them, a niche in the marketplace was found, and demand grew. In 1908, the Ford Motor Company produced the famous Model T Ford. Henry Ford's idea was to produce and market a motor car that the average person could afford to operate and maintain. The first Model T Ford sold for $850.00. Before 1908, it took 12 hours to assemble a Model T, but by 1914, new Model Ts had come off Ford's assembly line at the rate of one car every 24 seconds. With that speed, by 1915, the price of a Model T had dropped to $440.00 ($16,600 today), and by 1925, a Model T could be bought for $290.00 ($5,100), which was within reach of the average car buyer, and very cheap by today's standards. It's hard to find a running used car for $5,000 today, right?

For salespeople in 1914, the car would still have been a luxury. Fuel options were similar to today's access to electric vehicle charging stations. With weather conditions across the U.S., open-air vehicles presented challenges that would still be a decade away from solving. The road infrastructure across states was still being developed, and travel speeds meant lengthy trips when crossing hundreds of miles. Consider this would be an open-air vehicle with natural air conditioning and heat across dusty and unpaved roads.

By contrast, the train was a widely accepted mode of transportation for salespeople, and we'll examine this further as we move through the text below. Timothy B. Spears's book 100 Years on the Road—The Traveling Salesman in American Culture takes an in-depth and academic look at this period.

While the number of commuters and long-distance train travelers was at an all-time high before the 2020 COVID-19 pandemic and sank dramatically during that period, train ridership has continued to increase again over the last four years, making a resurgence across Amtrak and local commuter lines. As a salesperson in the city of Chicago, it was not uncommon for me to take the Metra into the city and walk to clients' offices with my printing samples and brochures. With the cost of parking and avoidance of traffic headaches on the expressways, I always found it more relaxing to make the most of my train experience. Of course, it also meant planning so that I could see as many people in a day as I could. Regional rail (Amtrak or others) makes similar sales opportunities accessible, especially in the Northeast Corridor. Travel between cities like Washington, D.C., Philadelphia, and New York is frequent. Again, not only does the cost of travel come into play today, but the convenience of accessing the internet and working while traveling, which is more difficult in a car stuck in traffic.

Commercial airlines didn't exist at the time of our 1914 book, and its invention would forever change how salespeople moved across the country, too. In the last report, in 2022, 5,193 commercial U.S. airports existed. According to the Centennial of Flight Commission, in 1914, there was a short-lived passenger service in South Florida. It used a converted waterside building for waiting passengers and the flying boats left from reinforced docks. Can you imagine being one of the first passengers? Would it be similar to the SpaceX opportunity to fly into space today? Well...maybe not as much, but it was quite revolutionary at the time. According to that same commission, by the end of World War I, the U.S. Army Air Service (USAAS) listed 980 official landing fields, but most were unsuitable for aircraft. Pilots had to navigate golf course bunkers, flags, and low ridges. Racetracks had tracks long enough for landing a plane but too short for taking off.

The following is a short list of the many inventions that were being perfected in 1914:

- Escalator
- TV and Television Broadcasts
- Indoor electric lighting
- Air Conditioners
- Motion Pictures
- Plastics
- Armored Tanks
- Vacuum cleaner

Notable Events of 1914

- WW I began with a telegram from Austria-Hungary to Serbia; the U.S. entered the war in October.
- Construction of the Lincoln Memorial in Washington, DC, begins 50 years after Lincoln's death.
- Panama Canal Opens

- Babe Ruth's debut in Major League Baseball with the Boston Red Sox.
- Born in 1914: Actor Alec Guinness (Star Wars), boxer Joe Louis, baseball great Joe DiMaggio

Points to Ponder

When you get in your vehicle today, which includes air conditioning, heat, automatic windows, and remote starting capabilities, consider how you might have gotten to see a client back in 1914. How much time would you have to allow for travel alone? What would you have to pack, and how does that differ from today? I believe the phone and transportation are the two most significant tools that have changed the sales profession over the last century. This period would have been an exciting time to enter the sales force, coupled with technological advancements and innovative new products and services. Take a moment and place yourself in the mid-1910s and consider your place as a salesperson; what does that feel like? Are you going to consider a different profession?

TERMS

House – Throughout the text, "the house" will be used to represent the word organization, company, or corporation. The idea of having a "home office" was not representative of remote workers or the gig economy but rather the company's central location. The term "house account" is still used today for sales accounts that aren't paid a commission or belong to the company, not a salesperson.

Interview – The sales "interview" took place when a salesman (salesperson) sat and asked the potential client relevant questions to ascertain their needs and desires. To a certain degree, the sales interview was bidirectional in that the client was also evaluating the credibility of the salesperson and their products/services.

Jobber – one who generally buys in quantities for the purpose of selling the same goods again without alteration to other dealers (wholesalers or retailers). If they sell to the end-user, they cease being a jobber and become a retailer. The term "Jobber" is rarely used in today's vernacular.

Big (Large) Man – The "big man" recognizes the owner or person of influence in business settings. Much like the term "Uncle Sam," which referred to the government looking out for us, the big man held a place of stature and, at times, was unapproachable due to the status they carried with them. The easiest way to translate throughout the text will be to consider CEO's or C-level executives.

Small Man – The words "small man" will serve two meanings within this discussion and work. The first is the inexperienced or untrained business professional. You will find the use of small man easy to spot throughout the text and may begin to see it coming in the following sentence. A second meaning occasionally refers to the common man or consumer; again, these terms will be simple to reconcile as you read.

Salesman – Masculine. Throughout the original book contained here, sales professionals will not only be referred to as "salesman" in nearly every case, but also the pronouns he, him, and his will be found in examples and stories. In the entire 588-page work, women are referenced 25 times, 19 as consumers, and only six as business/sales professionals. Within the commentary and points to ponder, salesperson, salespeople, or gender-neutral pronouns are incorporated.

Points to Ponder

My intent in providing a high-level look at **_Modern Business: Marketing Methods and Salesmanship_** is to provide a look at a historical document in the context of today's sales environment. Readers can insert themselves into the stories, incorporating gender influences as they choose, or at the very least, consider neutrality (they, them, we, us) pronouns into the mix. However, the reality was that the 19th Amendment to the U.S. Constitution, allowing women to vote nationally, would not be fully ratified until 1920. As you read the text, look for and consider alternate meanings or nuances in the language from 1914, have some fun, and embrace it.

Notes:

THE FIRST FIVE FOUNDATIONAL LESSONS FROM 1914

The following five segments are an independent introduction to our study of Marketing Methods and Salesmanship from 1914. These sections have been provided verbatim from the original text, and my brief commentary follows each. As suggested earlier, I will give you, the reader, an opportunity to learn lessons that are timeless sales truths through a historically significant piece.

⤜ Points to Ponder

Each of these five segments will set the tone for the remainder of the book. They were designed and are used as stand-alone and more lengthy lessons in my consultation with organizations. However, contained together in quick succession, I suggest you mark these sections and refer back to them as you read the additional compilation.

📖 FOUNDATIONAL LESSON #1

Excerpt from Part 2, Chapter I – Selling – It's place in the Field of Business

5. The salesman's dignified work. These various sides of the work of the salesman must be seen in order that the importance and dignity of his place in the business world may be appreciated. A century ago (1814), it was customary for inventors and men of rare genius to die in the poorhouse. For an inventor to be appreciated by his own generation was unusual; it took twenty-five or thirty years for the public to learn how to use his new article. Today, the inventor turns his article over to the man who can show people their need for it, and soon a rising industry has grown up around the inventor's idea. The modern salesman has accomplished in a year what was formerly the work of a generation.

In his work, he approaches men of varying importance; he must possess the ability to talk to the small man without condescension; he must meet the big man on his own level. To this work he must carry a thorough knowledge of his goods and the policies of his house and a capacity for intelligent initiative. In the eyes of the men he meets, he is not merely his house's representative—he is the house itself.

The modern salesman tries to be all that is implied by the term gentleman—both in appearance and character essentials. He looks upon a business engagement as a sacred trust. He guards jealously the confidence placed in him by his customer on the one hand and by his house on the other.

⌣ **Charlie's Commentary**

The modern salesperson plays a vital role in bridging innovation and industry, combining knowledge, integrity, and adaptability to earn trust and elevate their profession. Note that the second sentence above refers to a century earlier (1810s), yet here we are another 100+ years later talking about the profession of sales in similar terms.

Notes:

Excerpt from Part 2, Chapter 3 – The Selling Process – Preliminary to the Interview

25. Definition of a sale. From a legal point of view, to sell is to transfer property to another, or to contract to do so, for a valuable consideration, especially money. From a business point of view, the sale should, in addition, represent a profit to the owner of the goods. Not much salesmanship is required to give goods away or to sell below cost.

There is still another requisite. A sale, as a legitimate phase of commerce, should represent a profit or an advantage to the buyer. Some treatises on selling would lead one to believe that the average buyer is a putty-minded person before whom the scientifically instructed salesman makes a few mysterious passes and goes through certain occult moves, and thus simply hypnotizes him into signing an order whether he can use the commodity to advantage or not. The reminiscences of some salesmen would lead one to believe that most of their sales were made by a system of legerdemain that gave no consideration whatever to whether or not the buyer could use the goods to advantage. One wonders how men who were so easily persuaded to make disadvantageous purchases ever become sufficiently successful to be able to buy.

Of course, the truth of the matter is that the salesman has really taken the buyer's point of view, and, consciously or unconsciously, has made the buyer see that it is to his advantage to buy.

It is recognized today to be both poor ethics and bad business to sell one anything that he cannot use to advantage; and most salesmen realize that to overstock a dealer, although it may show fine powers of persuasion, will do no permanent good, to himself, his house, or his customer. A true sale, then, is one in which there is a profit three ways: to the house, to the buyer, and to the seller.

◔‿◔ Charlie's Commentary

An authentic sale is ethical and beneficial, ensuring profit and value for the seller, the buyer, and the business concern while avoiding manipulative or disadvantageous practices. It's a win-win-win situation. While written long before the stereotypical "slick" salesman as portrayed in the classic motion picture, Glengarry Glen Ross, the "horse trader" or flim-flam man gave the profession a poor reputation, even 100+ years ago. We can talk extensively about the buyer's journey today because information is readily available for the consumer with the click of a button, access to online reviews, price-shopping tools across nearly every industry, and purchasing power without even interaction with a sales professional.

Notes:

FOUNDATIONAL LESSON #3

Excerpt from Part 2, Chapter 3 – The Selling Process – Preliminary to the Interview

27. Preparation for the interview. Many interviews are opened smoothly by approaching a prospect on his "blind side"; that is, by talking to him of something in which he is deeply interested. Even though a salesman has a standard presentation, he will find it advantageous to modify it or add to it in such a manner as to tie his proposition closely to the prospect's interests. In other words, the salesman's talk must be suited to the prospect. This means that he should know as much as possible about the prospect before approaching him. Oftentimes, a great part of his knowledge must be secured by scrutinizing him as he crosses the office floor. He will secure some knowledge during the interview by getting the prospect to talk. The astute salesman gathers a great deal of valuable information before he ever faces his prospect, just as the general provides himself with topographical maps of the country over which his army is to operate.

28. Studying the prospect. Some men are opposed to change; others welcome new things. The college graduate looks at things differently from the self-made man. Some prospects will be young and ambitious to progress; others will be getting old and thinking of retiring. Some are wealthy and live modestly; others own a large house and drive a car. One plays golf; another is a tennis enthusiast or a baseball "fan." The nature of your individual business will dictate just what particular information you most desire. Bear in mind that after it is secured it will, in nine cases out of ten, be better not to use the information openly, but to draw it out by having the prospect tell it to you; or at least, to use it only indirectly.

Let us take a few examples. A representative of a New York publishing house was sent to induce the president of a great university to write a book. He immediately read the last book written by the educator. His opening remark then, when he called, was: "It is a pleasure to meet you. I have just completed the reading of your latest book." That put the interview on a favorable footing immediately.

A salesman calling upon an advertising manager whose firm's initial page in *The Saturday Evening Post* had appeared two weeks previously, immediately proceeded to congratulate the advertising manager upon having broken into the *Post* and commented upon the forcefulness of the copy used. It goes without saying that an advertising manager is proud of his first $4,000 page.

An insurance man had learned two things about one of his prospects: he was hostile to insurance and he had a son and a daughter at college. By talking specifically of the financial future of that particular son and daughter, instead of generally of the necessity of providing for one's family, he was able to remove the hostility.

A high-class salesman who does business with railroad presidents makes it a point to be thoroughly familiar with the railroad's last annual report and especially with the features of it that show marked gains.

A man who places exclusive agencies for a hardware specialty makes a practice of buying a key ring in each of the three or four hardware stores in a town. While he is being waited upon, he has an opportunity of looking around and getting a pretty definite impression. He then returns to the store that impresses him best and offers the agency.

⌣ Charlie's Commentary

Effective sales preparation requires understanding the prospect's interests, preferences, and background to tailor the approach, build rapport, and engage in meaningful, personalized interactions. The examples presented in section 28 show how information was used to benefit the sales process. Today, LinkedIn profiles coupled with simple Google search results will yield countless pieces of information that can be useful, provided the research is done. Unfortunately, those less professional unknowingly take shortcuts that fail to satisfy today's "house" requirements. Anecdotally, a third of all salespeople today are just getting into the business and need training and coaching. Another third are leaving the profession due to a lack of effort, ineffective training and motivation, misallocating resources, and aligning sales and marketing, which we'll look at briefly in section 161 below. The final third of sales professionals (in my opinion) continue to have a career that provides above-average compensation, benefits, and growth opportunities.

Excerpt from Part II, Chapter 10 – The Manufacturer's Campaign – Study of the Product

161. Importance of the marketing plan. No matter how good the advertising copy may be, no matter how effective the personal selling force, neither advertising nor salesmen can bring success to a business unless the plan of the campaign is right. What is the plan of campaign? It is definite advance knowledge of the methods to be used in marketing an article or the stock of a store, before the selling starts.

Opposed to a planned campaign are the hit-or-miss unplanned trials of this scheme or that, the vacillating, wavering attitude of the man who does not know exactly what he wants to do or how he wants to do it and who opens his mind and his purse to every will-o'-the-wisp scheme that is suggested to him by those who want his money. For instance, there is the small retail merchant who does not plan his advertising for a year in advance. He has no definite appropriation and is sold space not because it fits in with his marketing scheme but because of the personality and fluency of the solicitor.

Then, too, there is the manufacturer with no settled policy about trade channels. He may have been selling only to jobbers, but a big order from a retailer tempts him; he accepts it without thinking of the consequences, and trouble follows. There is also the advertiser who looks on advertising as a gamble. He puts his little bet on this medium or that, on this size space or on that preferred position, and sits back stoically to take his earnings or his losses with cynical expectation of the latter and only a gambler's hope of the former.

This is not advertising; it is plain gambling, and it is as seldom successful as it deserves to be. This does not necessarily imply that the "cut and try" method is wrong. The one best way is often found only by a process of elimination of the wrong ways. But if the whole so-called campaign consists in trying this and testing that, there is no campaign worthy of the name; the real campaign should start where the cutting and trying end.

＾＿＾ Charlie's Commentary:

A successful marketing campaign requires thorough planning and strategic foresight, avoiding unstructured, gamble-like approaches and instead focusing on tested and purposeful methods that align with long-term goals. Who among us today believes that a "fly by the seat of the pants" approach cuts it in our competitive environment today? If it was true in 1914, as suggested above, and we believe it today as much as we did back then, is this a timeless truth that will be confirmed 100 years from now? I would suggest that it is just as important as communication between marketing and sales. Having the two parts of your organization in lockstep potentially creates exponential results.

Excerpt from Part I, Chapter 11 – The Manufacturer's Campaign – Study of the Market

192. The study of competition. In connection with competition there are many questions to be asked and answered. First, how many competitors are there? The exact number can readily be learned from trade lists prepared by commercial agencies and trade publications. How long has each one been in business? What are the resources of each? Commercial agencies can also give information of this kind.

It is valuable to the manufacturer because it shows him the strength of the competitive army with which he must fight for business; he will hope to do his part in making new customers, but even for this new business he must compete with the other manufacturers in his field.

The modern businessman does not do much talking about his competitors; but he does business on definite knowledge of who they are, what they are doing, and what they are able to do in the field in which he is operating. To ignore competitors is to fight in the dark. Business is best conducted in the daylight of known competitive strength or weakness.

😊 **Charlie's Commentary**

A successful business strategy requires understanding competitors' strengths, weaknesses, and resources; operating without this knowledge is unthinkable today. Consider how someone would have to research competitors back in 1914 and recognize how much easier that would be today.

Keeping up with marketing efforts, pricing strategies, delivery schedules, and service levels is easier because we can access better online tools, including Artificial Intelligence applications that are emerging daily. Forty years ago, when I started my career in printing sales, combing through competitor catalogs could be incredibly time-consuming, and comparing quality or service levels was nearly impossible. I remember working at trade shows, which presented a unique opportunity to see several competitors' products and talk with their leadership, which it still does today. However, back then, it would be primary and firsthand information, whereas today, information about the company's history, leadership, and product details are available at every turn.

Notes:

SALES LESSONS

1914 to TODAY

NO!! I can't be bothered with any pesky salesman today.
I've got a battle to fight!!

LESSON 6 - AGENT, PEDALER OR CANVASSER? – WHO ARE YOU?

⌣
•‿•   **Charlie's Commentary:**

The following subsections of Marketing Methods and Salesmanship compare three types of salespeople between 1914 and today. Remember that mail-order businesses existed in 1914 and that large retailers like Sears provided both retail and a mail-order option as an innovation. They did so to get more products into the hands of more consumers, especially in rural settings. Automated online purchasing options (Alibaba, Amazon, Zappos, Barnes & Noble) have become competitive in the market through volume and technological advancements in delivery. Uber Eats and DoorDash are extensions of the first pizza delivery guys who brought us a hot pizza and allowed us to continue watching the football game on TV in the convenience of our home.

---

19. The agent. Commercially speaking, an **agent** is one who acts as the direct representative of a manufacturer, a jobber, or a retailer, who is compensated on some basis other than a straight salary, and who in the details of his activities is not responsible to his principal. The line between certain kinds of salesmen working on a commission basis and sales agents is difficult to draw distinctly. The agent, however, is an independent business man, often taking orders from his principal with respect to policy, profits, prices, terms of credit, etc., but yet retaining very large control over his own activities. Some of the additional characteristics of the agency relation are as follows: The agent usually, not always, sells by sample. Like the salaried employee of the principal, the agent binds the principal absolutely, within the scope of his agency, and does not assume individual liability for his acts. Goods shipped to the agent for delivery remain the property of the principal, who must bear all fire and other risks. The term agent is used very loosely in business. Sales managers are frequently incorrectly referred to as sales agents. Traveling salesmen are often agents in popular speech. These incorrect uses of the word should be avoided, and the term agent should be applied only to those whose activities come within the definition of the word.

21. The broker. The term broker is another name for commission merchant, and is the title applied to dealers trading on a commission basis in such lines as real estate, stocks, and bonds, etc. In the mercantile world brokers are sometimes found, but they are not a typical factor in modern industry.

26. The peddler. There are three modern types of the ancient itinerant merchant. The first of these is the peddler, who still supplies out-of-the-way communities with many of the necessities of life. The characteristic feature of his activities is that he carries his stock of goods with him, calls on those who may be interested in his wares, and makes immediate delivery of the goods that are purchased. This method of distribution, although useful and important in a primitive state of society, is obviously unsuited to modern conditions except in unusual cases. Its one advantage is that the customer can purchase at his own door. He is saved the necessity of doing anything except pay the price and receive the goods. The business of an itinerant dealer, however, must always be conducted on a small scale. Unless operated in connection with some other method of marketing, it can never develop to any great extent and, therefore, it can never seriously compete with that of distributors who are able to effect the economies that are always possible in large-scale business.

27. The canvasser. A second type of the modern itinerant merchant is the canvasser who solicits orders from house to house, but who does not carry his stock with him. The book-agent is an example of this type. Selling by means of personal solicitation of the consumer is appropriate when an article is so little known that its merits must be presented personally to each prospective purchaser, and when it is impossible or inexpedient to rely upon printed advertising to create a demand. Under such conditions, this method can be successfully employed. A business of this sort need not necessarily be conducted on a small scale. There are some exceedingly prosperous business houses that have made a careful study of this method of marketing and have built up national organizations of house-to-house solicitors. Publishers of books and maps, and manufacturers of stereoscopes, kitchen utensils, and a great variety of other goods do an immense business of this sort chiefly in rural and semi-rural districts; and some mail-order houses, like the Larkin Company, for example, have used this method of selling to supplement their catalog business. Nevertheless, its possibilities are limited. There is undoubtedly a popular prejudice against the house-to-house solicitor. His powers of salesmanship have so often been enlisted in the support of articles of questionable merit that even the canvasser with a strictly reputable article to offer often finds his usefulness limited by reason of the prejudice that exists against his selling methods.

28. The specialty salesman. A third type of the dealer who takes his wares directly to the consumer may be termed a specialty salesman, for lack of a better name. The difference between him and the house-to-house canvasser is principally one of degree and not of method. Instead of calling upon everybody, the specialty salesman carefully selects his prospective customers and centers his attention upon them. It seems a far cry from the persistent solicitor for "Lives of the Presidents" to the highly paid commercial ambassador who obtains a railroad's order for fifty thousand dollars' worth of supplies, but so far as selling methods are concerned, the two types of salesmen must be placed in approximately the same class. They both deal directly with the consumer, and they both ignore the retail store and the mail-order method of selling. Both are just modern types of the old itinerant merchant. The one adopts this method of marketing because he believes it good policy to do so—the other, because the nature of his goods demands it.

Points to Ponder

- Does your organization or those you work with lean to one or more of these sales methods?

- What factors make that decision for them or you?

- What differences are there today when compared with 1914?

- What will be different in the next 20, 50, 100 years regarding how sales take place?

- How has technological advancement affected cold-call canvassing?

- Who do you want to represent your company today?

LESSON 7 – CUSTOMER RELATIONS MANAGEMENT (CRM) SYSTEMS AND INDEX CARDS

˜ ˘   Charlie's Commentary

Today's modern Client Relations Management (CRM) systems serve the same purpose as the traditional card index (3 ½" x 5" or 4" x 6" purchased through a variety of sources), helping salespeople track customer interactions, financial details, and personal information to maintain continuity and strengthen relationships over time. However, the differences in efficiency, effectiveness, and connections to marketing capabilities are worlds apart.

I personally had a Rolodex (still available today), which included information contained on business cards (often stapled to the Rolodex card). Each card had additional information obtained over a period of time. It could consist of family names, how I was introduced, or the next steps in the sales process. Using a tickler file with cards, reminders are kept in calendar order by month and by date, 1-31. This method added a time component for when the subsequent follow-up should take place. The way it worked was that a stack of cards would be in each month, January – December, based on when you thought you should follow up; some months had more cards than others. At the beginning of each month, I would then distribute them into a 1-31 file showing which I should follow up early in the month, in the middle of the month, or at the end. After the call/visit, the card would be placed in the appropriate follow-up month.

Today, CRM systems make this far more sophisticated and automated by using fields within the software to track your first visit, next follow-up date, anticipated closing date, and deployment date. The software has multiple note fields, allowing you to capture the essence of your conversation, attach proposals or correspondence via email, and identify the value of the opportunity. SalesForce.com, HubSpot, and many other CRM solutions allow for fields such as likelihood to close (percentage) and the sale stage (Initial contact, demonstration, evaluation, negotiation). Companies and salespeople can track the close as a win or loss with reasons, evaluate closing ratios, and focus on the reasons they win or lose to better prepare for the next opportunity. Let's look at what they did in 1914...

---

30. Using a card index What has been said applies primarily to the salesman who sees his customer for the first time. Unless he sees his customers regularly and at short intervals, however, they are likely to assume something of the nature of new prospects every time he calls upon them. A salesman who calls upon his customer only once in three or four months and depends upon his memory is likely to forget more or less important details.

For that reason, many salesmen keep a simple card index of their customers. Upon each card is kept a record of the man's financial standing, the business done with him on previous occasions, and various items of personal information gained during the first and succeeding interviews. These cards are gone over before each call.

Points to ponder:

- Thinking about CRM solutions, are you using one, and if so, which one?

- Is it integrated throughout your sales department, marketing, or company?

- How can you use it better to get personal with your clients?

- What information is most important? To what extent do you keep the information current?

Notes:

LESSON 8 - USING THE TELEPHONE

‿ ‿
ᵔ Charlie's Commentary

As shown in the following section, the phone's best use was to gain an appointment and often as a last resort. It is suggested that it is easier for prospective clients to turn down a salesperson on the phone than in person. As many salespeople today have found, leaving voice messages and following up accordingly is an art. I wrote two blog posts on this subject Voicemail - Are you returning those messages? and Voicemail - Are your messages being returned? and a podcast: How to Makes Sales With Voicemail. Statistically, only one in twenty (5%) phone voice messages are returned today. This is a staggering statistic on several levels. Responsiveness is a lost art, and promptly returning calls will be rewarded handsomely.

The text below assumes that the salesperson will see the decision maker in person; how different is that today? As shown in #55 below, selling a telephone system based on features and functionality doesn't work, even when the innovation was extremely visible. Pay close attention to how the seasoned salesperson takes a different approach and consider how that might play out in your industry and with your clients.

34. Use of telephone Courteous persistence gets many an interviewer on a favorable basis. The average prospect feels rather conscience stricken and ashamed of continually turning a man down without a hearing. Very often, it is possible to reach a man over the telephone, when he cannot be reached in person in his office. If he can be gotten on the 'phone, a short, effective canvas for a definite appointment should be made. The telephone is a sort of last resort, however, and should never be used when it is possible to reach the prospect in person. It is much easier for the man being called to turn the salesman down over the 'phone than it would be if they were face to face. Some houses instruct their salesmen never to do business over the 'phone because of the disadvantage at which it places them.

55. Talking customers, not telephones.   There was a stage in the development of the telephone business when it was a simple matter to persuade a businessman to install a telephone, but a different and more difficult thing to sell him an equipment that was adequate. There was, at that time, a department store in Illinois that had but one wire with two extensions, one on each floor of the store. The telephone people were convinced that this equipment was inadequate, but they had failed on several occasions to make the proprietor recognize that fact.

Finally one of the big commercial men of the company came down from Chicago to see what he could do. His first words to the merchant were: "I have come to talk to you about the service you are giving to your customers." He then proceeded to show how people who wanted to order goods over the 'phone, found it difficult to do so because they were kept waiting while others talked over the one wire. Many times, he pointed out, this delay caused a decision not to bother ordering by 'phone, but to buy later in person, with the possible result that the trade went to another store. If the customer were sufficiently patient to wait, she explained the object of her call to the clerk answering the 'phone on the first floor, explained it again when she connected on the second story extension, and, after holding the wire while the proper clerk was called, she was obliged to go over the whole matter a third time. Meanwhile the clerk downstairs had been called from his work, the first clerk who had answered the upstairs extension had been disturbed, and he or someone else had then to go after a clerk in the department to which the order belonged, and he probably had to travel the length of the floor to reach the telephone. All this time customers in the store were being neglected and kept waiting because the clerk who should have been at a certain station was out of his department answering the telephone.

The principal theme in his talk was customers and not telephones. The customer was a subject in which the merchant was greatly interested, so he asked: "What would you suggest?" The telephone man suggested two trunk lines, a switchboard, an extension for each department, and an advertisement in the paper that they were especially well equipped to give the customer the best kind of service on telephone orders. The contract was signed immediately. Throughout the interview the salesman had taken the "You" attitude. **(note: see Lesson #11, section 54)**

Points to Ponder

- If it was hard in 1914 to get someone on the phone, what makes it challenging today?

- What is your phone strategy? Have you given it enough thought? Do you have a plan?

- Using the sale of the phone system, for example, in #55, what made the difference to the prospective client? What brought the prospect to a decision?

- If you are struggling to close enough opportunities, have you considered who benefits from the conversation, you or the client?

Notes:

LESSON 9 – APPROACHING OTHERS

⌒ ⌒
⌒   **Charlie's Commentary**

Over my lengthy sales career, I have been blessed to work with some extremely large companies like State Farm Insurance, L.A. Fitness, and Walmart. Someone once told me that the most influential leaders of large companies still put their pants on the same way I do, one leg at a time. This mindset, along with the gumption (yes, I'm choosing to use that word) to find a way to speak with them, put me at a distinct advantage because, in the fields that I was in, fewer salespeople were willing to do the work necessary to reach the right decision makers.

In the case of a large retailer, our company had been responding to requests for proposals (RFPs) that came frequently but with uniform requirements. I recognized that these RFPs seemed to cause a great deal of overhead to produce, evaluate, and select the winner. Besides, we had to do the work of responding each time as well.

Our company had won several awards, and I decided to take a bold approach before the next one was released. I invited the primary contact to lunch and began asking questions about their processes and how they awarded service contracts. They were generally happy with our company's service and price on the project, which involved installing low-voltage cabling for fire alarms and security systems.

When I asked the following question, I believe the buyer recognized the difference between a professional salesperson and a less experienced one. I asked this: "If we were able to standardize our pricing such that it met your requirements, as we've done in the past, AND we could guarantee that your project would be placed in top priority with our best installation team, would you provide us with a contract for the next X number of locations within our geography?" One sentence captured it all...in baseball terms, game over! Zig Ziglar said, "You will always get what you want if you help enough other people get what they want." The client got our best team at a consistent price, with a guarantee that we'd meet their stringent deadlines, AND we would do so without the hassles associated with quoting the project each time. Winner, winner, chicken dinner.

I want to share briefly the topic that follows in section 37 and the term "cooperation." Cooperation = Referrals.

In countless sales situations, millions of successful salespeople have asked a friend or contact to make an introduction on their behalf. This is the most recommended strategy for all the lessons in this book. Would you like to cold call a company with a person you've never met or have ever heard of you, or would you prefer to open up your call or email as follows: "Mrs. Jones, I understand that you've done business with my good friend and colleague, Mr. Smith. Bob suggested that I contact you directly because you value relationships and may need the solution I represent. Could we meet for a brief 15 minutes to get acquainted and for me to learn more about your specific challenges in the _____ area?"

LinkedIn and your client base should be sufficient to create enough referrals to keep you busy for some time. However, I will suggest that this mindset should be grounded in every new relationship. A raving fan mindset suggests that if someone likes or loves your service, they would be willing to introduce others on your behalf. We do it all the time, don't we? For a deeper dive, I can highly recommend Bob Burg's book *Endless Referrals and The Referral Engine* by John Jansch. Both books can help you set up a program that is the best that a professional salesperson can acquire.

CHAPTER III – THE SELLING PROCESS – PRELIMINARY TO THE INTERVIEW

31. Getting to see the buyer. A salesman who had sent his name in to a large buyer received the reply that the buyer did not wish to see him. "Tell your boss," he quickly instructed the office boy, "that I already knew he didn't want to see me; it is I who wish to see him"; and the story goes that he saw the buyer. If he did, he accomplished quite an important thing; for it is not until the salesman has been able to get face to face with his prospect, that his appearance, personality, knowledge of his goods or the best talking point he may have at his tongue's end, can do the least good.

There is little trouble, of course, in seeing the proprietor of the small retail store. It is seldom that any difficulty is experienced in getting to see any man in the average manufacturing concerns in the smaller cities. A great many of the largest concerns and largest men, too, make it a point to see that every salesman is received courteously and given an audience. The United Cigar Stores Company have issued specific orders to this effect in their general offices in New York. The Chalmers Motor Company have displayed in their reception room a large sign, apologizing for any delay that may occur in granting the salesman an audience and inviting him, meanwhile, to peruse the papers from his own hometown or to use their telephone. Both things are provided. In a great many cases where the formality of giving your name to an office boy or telephone operator must be gone through, the invariable answer to the operators' "Mr. Blank to see you" is "Tell him to come right in." The average man's natural curiosity, coupled with his aversion to walking outside to see you, will prompt that.

37. Using cooperation to see the prospect. There is nothing more valuable to the salesman than cooperation—cooperation of customers, friends, and even of other salesmen. It is especially valuable in the matter of getting interviews. It makes the securing of an interview under favorable auspices a simple matter even with those who are most difficult to see. The prospect is prepared to give an interested hearing to the salesman's whole story out of courtesy to the friend who sent him. The fact that he has come recommended has likewise created confidence in him.

The live salesman, particularly in specialty lines, is continually on the lookout for helps of this sort, for they represent to him the lines of least resistance. As he goes from town to town, he picks up here and there a card of introduction from some brother salesman to one of that salesman's particularly intimate customers. He secures letters of introduction and of commendation of his proposition from one town to another and from one man to another. He secures from every man to whom he sells the names of some friends who are, for example, likely to be interested prospects. The best possible source of prospects for an automobile salesman is the man who has bought a car, is enthusiastic about it, has been boosting it to his friends, and is sufficiently friendly to the salesman to tell him who among them are thinking of cars or can afford them. He then secures definite permission to use the customer's name with these new prospects. This gives him a strong entering wedge: "I interested your friend, Mr. Brown, in my proposition yesterday and he asked me to make it a point to see you before I left town." He uses another angle on this by getting the man he has just sold to telephone any friends who are possible prospects and tell them that he is coming. He is careful, in using this latter method, to make sure that his man does not endeavor to give the friend a selling talk over the 'phone, but merely announces that the salesman is going to drop in. Cooperation of this kind enables the salesman to occupy his time in interviewing and not in seeking interviews.

Points to Ponder

- In section 36 it is suggested that it is easier to talk to smaller businesses, but that more significant business concerns (large men) still met regularly with salespeople. What is different today, and how have C-level business professionals and owners insulated themselves from a salesperson's request for a meeting? Does that surprise you?

- Are you seeking meetings with the decision maker?

- Do you have a referral strategy, as section 37 recommends? Are you regularly asking for "cooperation" from customers, friends, and even other salesmen?

- What HAS NOT changed between referral strategies today and back in 1914?

Notes:

LESSON 10 – ANNOUNCING YOURSELF (ELEVATOR TALK)

˜ ⌣ **Charlie's Commentary**

As important today as it was back then, there is no substitute for a good first impression. Based on what is shared in this section, you can see that in 1914, it was crucial to differentiate yourself from other salespeople. In looking at these three brief paragraphs, the young professional reading the words would have some homework to do. He (or she) would need to polish their introduction, practice it in front of others, including their boss or a surrogate, and take it for a test drive. Vince Lombardi famously said, "Practice does not make perfect. Only perfect practice makes perfect."

I had the opportunity to have an elevator involved in a prospective sale situation. Being polite, coming off of an elevator in 1989, I made brief small talk with a fellow elevator rider who happened to be going to the same place I was. I allowed her to get off the elevator first, was polite in holding the door for her, and greeted her with a smile. After she sat down in the waiting room, it was my turn to introduce myself to the prospective medical practice. I spoke to the office manager in a way that made the woman listen in on the conversation; she took notice. As I walked past her to leave, she engagingly looked at me. "Did I overhear correctly that you work for a printing company?" she asked. "Yes, ma'am, that's correct; why do you ask?"

The woman stood up, gave me her card, and told me that her company was unhappy with their current printer and had begun entertaining other options. She asked for my card and we set an appointment for the following week. She was in charge of buying all the printing for a retail furniture company, and after my first meeting, she placed what would be the first of many lucrative and sizable orders over the next three years. It was a lesson for me to be respectful, present my products well at all times, and never be surprised about where the next client may come from.

---

38. Individuality in announcing oneself. The large department stores of New York and Chicago have very rigid rules as to how salesmen shall announce themselves and at what time they shall be seen. As practically every house in every line has one of its men call on these stores, the number of salesmen in and out during the day is enormous. A rather arbitrary selection is made of those who will be seen and comparatively few reach the buyers of their lines. The question of how to proceed to secure an audience under these circumstances was frequently brought up in the authors' lecture courses by salesmen who were meeting these conditions every day. As a result, the merchandising man of one of the largest New York department stores was interviewed in collecting the material for this text. In his house, the salesman is obliged to give his name and his line and this information a girl writes on a regular form.

There seems little chance for individuality here. When asked as to that, however, the merchandising man said: "Oh, yes, a few of the salesmen who come in show considerable ingenuity. For example, I received a slip one day which the salesman had evidently taken away from the girl and upon which he had written: 'The first day it was on the floor, Marshall Field sold twenty-five of the models I want to show you now.' You may be sure he got in," he concluded. It is quite natural that the busiest buyer imaginable would have time for a proposition like that.

The same merchandising man brought out another point. A friend of his was selling cloaks and suits, and had the usual trouble reaching buyers of the large department stores. "Your house sells mourning goods," he advised. "The cloak and suit salesmen who call on us are legion. There are very few calling on us with a line of mourning goods. Instead of the 'cloaks and suits' on your card now, place 'mourning goods.' So few men sell mourning goods that you will almost invariably be seen. After you have secured an audience on your specialty, there is nothing to prevent your 'talking cloaks and suits, also.'" It would seem, then, that the obstacles to seeing a large department store buyer are not insurmountable to the salesman of some ingenuity and originality.

39. The approach proper. Let us suppose, now, that the salesman is in. He is crossing the space between the office door and the prospect's desk. The prospect, at this point, is sizing up the salesman, just as the salesman is sizing up the prospect. Here is the place of first impressions. The salesman decides, in those few seconds, whether he can take advantage of a good first impression or will have a bad one to fight. He is deciding whether the prospect will devote the first few moments of the interview to an endeavor to shunt him off or to an effort to make him feel at home. To a certain extent, he is deciding whether he shall dominate or be dominated. There must be no attitude of servility or idea that he is really trespassing upon the prospect's time. There must be a sincere feeling of equality and dignity and a realization of the importance of his mission. The confident man with a mission is known the minute he steps into a room.

Points to Ponder

- How often have you written or rewritten your opening elevator talk or, as Bob Burg calls it, your "benefit statement"? Does it include a compelling call to action (engagement) with the prospective client or concisely share your value proposition?

- When was the last time you revisited how you introduce yourself? Is it time to do so again?

- In section 39, it is suggested that confidence is vital to the initial meeting. Do you agree? If so, what do you do that demonstrates confidence in your product or service, your company, and, most importantly, yourself? How is confidence different than domination?

Notes:

LESSON 11 – COMMANDING ATTENTION

⌒‿⌒ **Charlie's Commentary**

There is much to unpack in this lengthy, five-segment lesson. Listening is essential for your prospective client because there are so many distractions today. We have smartphones with notifications for texts, emails, and posts from various social media or newsfeeds. If our computers are on, we each likely have multiple windows open, including Outlook and personal email; we also have stock market ticklers running in the background, home Ring videos alerting us of people coming to our homes while we're at work, and the latest NFL player updates pop up allowing us to make better decisions in our Fantasy Football leagues. Of course, some people have an Apple watch telling them how many steps they've taken, what their heart rate is, and when they need to eat a snack...oh, and all the while providing the same updates received on our other devices. If we consider the highest-level decision makers (C-suite), they have additional time constraints with leadership meetings, business travel, vacations, holidays, and a myriad of other responsibilities. Is it any wonder why the salesperson can't reach the decision-maker?

Some examples and stories relate to the 1914 period, but I'm sure that as you read them, you can see how they may be slightly changed by using products or services from today. One thing is certain: focusing on understanding the client and their desires is at the heart of it all.

A realtor friend shared a timeless story about homebuyers. She said listening to the couple buying the home is the key to their interest in a specific home during the showing. When, not if, the couple begins seeing themselves in the house, that alone oftentimes seals the deal. This realtor said that she listens explicitly for comments between spouses like: "Our couch will look good in front of this fireplace" or "My 60" TV will fit on that wall." I'll contend that if you (the salesperson) are distracted by emails on their phone, incoming calls, or other things that get in the way of being "present," they are likely to miss those essential cues.

**Excerpt From Chapter IV:
Selling Process—The Interview**

40. Attention: its nature. Psychologists tell us that the mind is under a continual bombardment of ideas, all trying to make an impression upon it. The activities of a man's business going on about him; the people around him; the ideas that he has in mind to work out; the train of thought started by some object on which his vision rests; to say nothing of such commonplace things as his morning mail, papers on his desk, and his telephone; all constantly clamor for his attention. And what is more, one or several of these things insistently command that attention. The prospect, therefore, does not sit around with his mind a blank, calmly waiting for someone or something to capture his attention without a struggle. The salesman enters a field already well occupied and must fight for the undivided attention which is essential to a successful sale. He must, by his personality, his proposition, and especially by his opening remarks, eliminate all competitors for that attention and hold the field alone.

41. Conditions favorable to attention. Since it is so elusive, the salesman should not seek the prospect's attention at a time when other strong claims are pressing upon it. If the prospect is really too busy to give his attention, it is to the salesman's advantage to make a definite appointment and call again. If he is waiting to attend to some important business, the salesman should avoid being granted a short five or ten minutes of his time, for the prospect will find it impossible to give him any serious attention, since that will already have been claimed. It goes without saying, of course, that the salesman should be convinced of the sincerity of the prospect and should not allow himself to be put off with mere excuses.

The astute salesman will never break in upon a retailer when he is engaged with a customer. Nor will he stand waiting for any length of time where the retailer may be disturbed by his presence. To the man in business, selling is more interesting always than buying. In the case of men who usually transact business sitting at a desk, it is a distinct disadvantage for the salesman to present the proposition while he stands. When the prospect is comfortably seated in his chair, his body will cease its clamor and competition with the salesman's idea for his attention. A positive suggestion to sit down at his desk should be made as indicated in the last chapter. The presence of others close to the prospect should be avoided if possible, because those about him will distract his attention; and furthermore, most men are rather shy about being persuaded to buy anything in the presence of friends.

A salesman should never attempt to talk to a man who is not listening, who is writing a letter, or occupying himself in any other way. He should not attempt to compel attention by loud, fast, or feverish talking. One of the best specialty salesmen in the country, when he met a situation of this kind, was wont to sit back and ask in a very dignified way, "Does this interest you, Mr. Prospect?" The answer almost invariably was an apologetic "Yes." His idea was that in order to be successful, he would have to dominate the interview at every point. He preferred to lose the sale in a clean battle for the domination of the interview, rather than to allow the prospect to dominate him and give him but a scant measure of attention.

The ideal conditions under which to secure a prospect's undivided attention are, to be alone with the prospect, to have him comfortable, and to have absolute quiet.

44. Transferring attention to goods. The first attention that a salesman secures will be directed to himself. It is a peculiar psychological fact that any impression, favorable or unfavorable, that the salesman makes upon the prospect in his approach will be transferred to the goods, when attention is diverted to them. Without thinking much about it, the prospect assumes that a reliable house will not be represented by a poorly dressed or careless salesman. The article of good quality would seem to call for a man of quality. The converse, then, is also true; the big-calibered salesman will suggest a reliable house; the man of quality will suggest an article of quality.

The salesman must divert the prospect's attention from himself to his goods if the sale is to progress. Any exaggeration of dress or manner, a loud voice or violent gestures will make this difficult. A gentlemanly, low-voiced salesman with an easy manner can easily divert his prospect's attention to the goods by placing them before him or making some strong, positive statement regarding them.

Any unnaturalness of speech or manner is likely to delay this diversion of the prospect's attention. The salesman who uses a standard presentation and has not made it his own so that he can deliver it naturally, will find it difficult to get his prospect's attention to the article sold. A great many of the so-called clever openings have this same defect.

Strange as it may seem, the man who talks easily and well is likely to meet the same difficulty. It is not uncommon for a prospect to become wary of the smooth talker who calls upon him for the evident purpose of getting an order. A mild gray-haired man who was after a large machinery order said very early in his interview with the company's president: "I'm not much of a salesman; you see, I have been on the buying end nearly all my life and I find myself constantly taking the buyer's point of view." It was not until he walked out with the order in his pocket that those who had heard him began to realize just how much of a salesman he really was.

47. Attention through curiosity. Curiosity is a strong incentive to giving a proposition undivided attention. The opening remarks of a great many able salesmen are framed to arouse a healthy curiosity in the prospect. The exclusive agency man referred to in the last chapter would return to the store that he had picked for his agency and, approaching the proprietor, would ask: "Do you remember me?" "Yes," would come the answer, "I sold you a key ring this morning." Thereupon the salesman would remark that the key ring business had been pretty good in that town, and holding out his hand, would display those he had bought. The proprietor would naturally want to know if he was making a collection. "No," would be his reply, "my firm sent me here with your name as that of the representative merchant in this town. My key ring experiment has substantiated that information."

From that point he would use another strong lever for the getting of attention. "I am here," he would continue, "to secure your opinion of our new merchandising plan, which is of particular interest to live hardware merchants. I should appreciate your going over our proposition and telling me what you think of it." A prospect finds it very hard to refuse to listen to a salesman's story if all that is desired at the end is a candid opinion. It is needless to say that this opinion is usually favorable and is voiced by the prospect's putting his name on the dotted line.

Returning to the motive of curiosity in securing attention; a salesman one day stepped into the office of the general manager of a large Western telephone company. "Mr. Manager," said he, "supposing I were to come to you with a pencil"—drawing one from his pocket—"with which your clerk could write down numbers"—and suiting the action to the word, he wrote down several numbers of four figures each—"and after doing so, could find the total of those numbers right here at the top of the pencil. That would be a wonderful pencil, would it not?" The manager had to admit that it would.

"Well," resumed the salesman, "I haven't a pencil that will do that, but here is a writing machine that will." And forthwith he produced from his case a typewriter with an adding attachment and proceeded with a demonstration.

54. The "you" attitude. Above all, it must be remembered in getting attention, that the prospect is more interested in himself and his business than he is in the salesman or the salesman's business. The latter's opening, therefore, should always approach the proposition from the prospect's point of view. Any talk about the salesman or the salesman's house that fails to get the prospect into the story is going to leave him cold and uninterested. We said previously that salesmanship was the taking of the prospect's viewpoint and swinging him around to ours. The talk to a jobber should take him on an imaginary selling trip and picture him selling the commodity offered to his customers. To the retailer a picture of himself reselling the commodity over his counter at a profit, is bound to be interesting. The customer must be pictured as enjoying the article. The prospect for an automobile should see himself, in his mind's eye, speeding along in the sunshine to the admiration of his friends and acquaintances. By painting a picture and putting the prospect in it, the salesman stands the best chance of securing undivided attention.

Points to Ponder

- Do you draw attention to yourself in the early stages of the sales process? What can you do to return the attention back to your product or service?

- There are several examples of using curiosity to draw attention in the sections above. Does one stand out over another for you? How can you foster additional curiosity in your sales presentations?

■ What habits can you change to make yourself a more attentive salesperson? Less distracted? More engaging in personal conversations?

■ The "you" attitude describes explicitly taking on the client's viewpoint. How have you done it recently, and how can you focus more on doing so going forward?

■ Can you picture yourself selling cars in 1914? Have car sales changed so much in 110 years? How does this apply to YOUR business and sales approach?

Notes:

LESSON 12 – ATTENDING TO THE CLIENT
(TRADE SHOWS, SHOWROOMS, SAMPLE ROOMS)

ʕ •̀ ω •́ ʔ **Charlie's Commentary**

If you have ever attended a trade show or association conference, you understand that they often occur in large hotel ballrooms; they are frequently held in a convention center with one or more hotels connected to it. This makes it easy for those displaying companies to stay in the hotel rooms, which earns revenue for those hotels. Additionally, attendees have access to food in the hotel's restaurant(s), which is both convenient and profitable for the hotel owner. Having everything in one place reduces the travel for everyone concerned, which in turn reduces the friction of attendees and oftentimes reduces travel costs if these hotels or convention centers are in close proximity to the airport or interstate highways.

To pick an easy example with car dealerships today, mega showrooms or "auto malls" have been created for the customer's ease. With many dealerships and models to choose from in a very condensed space, oftentimes at an intersection of busy highways, shopping malls, or near a variety of restaurants in highly dense population centers, the buying experience is enhanced for all concerned. A bonus for many auto malls is that they are located near rail lines for easier vehicle delivery.

In the heyday of train travel, traveling salespeople relied on sample rooms or showrooms within hotels that allowed them to share their product offerings with retail buyers or resellers of other types. Still, these convenient locations often shared their product with the general public. Oftentimes, they were convenient within walking distance of the train depot; it was easier for the large trunks to be hauled from the train to the hotel. With the next stop on the rail line a day or two away, the salesperson could have a good meal, have the convenience of a nice room, and invite others to see them in one location. In 1914, this rural practice was commonplace for quite some time. With urban sprawl and larger cities attracting more attention, traveling salespeople had to be more efficient and rely on their sales skills to attract potential customers.

---

51. Trunk lines and sample rooms. Let us discuss now, for a moment, the case of the salesman carrying a "trunk line"—to use the vernacular—a line which involves the carrying of one or more large trunks of samples. Securing the prospect's attention here, to the whole line at least, involves persuading him to visit the salesman's sample room at the hotel, unless the salesman desires to bring his sample trunks up to the door and can secure the prospect's consent. This is not usually practicable in small towns because the salesman will want several buyers to see his line, and because there is no space in most small stores where he could open his trunks. In the department stores in the larger cities it is not unusual for sample rooms to be provided where the salesman can display his line just as he would in a hotel sample room; but even here an appointment must be secured.

There are two great advantages in getting the buyer down to the hotel. First, the opportunities for displaying the line are likely to be better; and second, the buyer is away from his place of business and the possibility of interruption from his employees.

Points to Ponder

- Can you imagine yourself traveling by train, hauling a large trunk filled with samples, and displaying them at your hotel? Does that sound more or less appealing than how you sell your product or service today?

- What challenges do you face with getting your product or service in front of prospective clients today? In what ways can you be creative and do so more effectively?

- Would having your product on display right next to your competitor be frightening to you? Would you be more or less cautious about sharing the features/functionality if you knew your competitor would have that knowledge? What would you do with the knowledge that you gained about your competitor?

Notes:

LESSON 13 – TESTING OUT SALES METHODS

⌣ Charlie's Commentary

You may be asking, "Why didn't we start here? This is another foundational truth." I chose to include it in the latter portion of the lessons because we hope not to have to do this. We hope that the company (house) has already figured it out on our behalf, and all we need to do is pick up the phone, see the client, and share our solution.

If you've been selling the same thing for a long time, you've seen changes in the market, the clients, and the technology available for you to use. When PowerPoint came out, handwritten flip charts went by the wayside, right? As whiteboards entered the market, you no longer needed a chalkboard to write. And when whiteboards became "smart," we could incorporate the internet with live product demonstrations and videos.

Today, software demonstrations lead to trial licenses, allowing the customer to take the app for a test drive. Mattress salespeople have been demonstrating beds similarly for a hundred years, right? What better way to check out the feel than to jump from bed to bed, but the really good salesperson is exploring the client's sleep habits, current bedding, hotel experiences, and personal preferences between partners to see if dual-sided beds are the best option.

173. Testing out selling methods. In the case of a new proposition, the most important thing in developing the sales organization is to secure a few men who can test out the details of the selling plan previously determined upon, make such changes in it as may be necessary, suggest proper equipment, work out an effective selling talk and devise the details of personal selling methods; and who can, above all, set a pace and show what can be done in the way of sales.

This will be true in staple lines as well, because even here field methods must be worked out if the new proposition is to compete successfully with older lines. For example, a hardware concern, putting out a newly invented and ingenious knife sharpener, met with but little success in the way of sales by merely turning the proposition over to their regular salesmen as another item in the line. One of the best men was put on the proposition to make a study of it and work out successful selling methods. He found that in the few cases where sales had been made the knife sharpener had not moved from the dealer's counter. He worked out a method of taking the knives of the dealer and his clerks and sharpening them with a few deft moves. When he had aroused their interest, he encouraged them to try it on his knife. He then secured a good-natured but sincere promise from the dealer and his clerks to make at least twenty-four demonstrations to each dozen of the sharpeners. His second visit to the dealers a week later revealed the fact that the sharpeners moved rapidly under the new method and that the dealers, as a consequence, were ready to reorder. This method, passed on to the other salesmen of the concern, resulted in every one of them being able to make large sales of the sharpener. A great many sales opportunities are missed because special selling methods of this sort are not worked out.

Points to Ponder

- Using the example of the knife sharpener, give thought to the evolution of your sales demonstration or sales process. Did it take longer or shorter to figure out and hone in on? How much valuable time was delayed or saved?

- Have you tested your strategies enough to know that your current process is good?

- What other processes within your organization lend themselves well to this type of testing?

Notes:

LESSON 14 – DRIVING DEMAND –
STAPLES VS SPECIALTIES

⌒‿⌒ **Charlie's Commentary**

This section speaks for itself and provides some examples that are relatable today. Elizabeth Allen talks extensively about the process of *Driving Demand* in her book by the same name. Much has been written today about clients' sales methods and buying trends for many years. The fact that 1914 leaders looked at breaking products into staples vs. specialties is easy to see. Innovative new solutions were coming around quickly, and while "discretionary income" was still not abundant, there were those who could afford what today may be considered luxury items. The concept of middle-class consumerism would arrive in the post-depression and post-WWII eras; the boom would be seen in the 1950s and 1960s, and services would join product solutions as convenience allowed for milk delivery, dry cleaning services, and the fast-food phenomenon.

In observing salespeople for over 40 years, I've noticed a trend that follows personality types, education levels, and circumstances, leading to someone's choice in sales. Some people naturally feel more comfortable with smaller ticket items that are reordered more regularly. In contrast, others prefer the larger ticket items (oftentimes durable goods) where the commission amount or compensation can be significantly higher for each item sold. Similarly, some salespeople are drawn to a product with features/functionality that can be demonstrated, while others prefer selling services like bank lending, financial services, insurance, or the like. Still, others find that focusing on a single product/service is best for them, while others gravitate to large lines with many different products or offerings. Why is that?

My experience says that some salespeople are more or less risk-averse than others. Oftentimes, it has to do with what solution they initially land on. My college roommate started with an independent insurance agency and stayed in that field for his entire life. Using expertise to further their standing can also lend itself well to this and many other professions. Coaching high school baseball may lead to a small college position and, eventually, a D-1 gig. Similarly, using my experience in a small printing company increased my credibility to work at larger manufacturing firms, which in turn landed me owning my own printing business. However, it is important to recognize that there are many transferable skills between types of sales. While fear of change factors into many salespeople's decision to stay, plenty reinvent themselves throughout their careers. As we will see in just a few pages from now, that experience can lend itself to other leadership roles outside of sales.

---

18. Staples and specialties. By far the most important classification of selling is that based on the nature of the commodity sold; namely, whether it be a staple or a specialty. A staple may be defined as a commodity necessary to carry on the primary functions of living under existing standards. Sugar, coffee, cotton goods, and shoes are staples. Since there is a universal demand for such commodities as these, it is not required of the salesman to create a demand before the sale can be made.

A specialty may be defined as an article for which there may exist a potential demand or for which it is possible to create a demand, but which has not been generally incorporated into the people's standard of living. Phonographs, conducted tours, and automobiles are examples of specialties. People must be educated to demand these things and a desire for them must be created in each individual sale.

19. Selling specialties. As the definitions would indicate, the bulk of the expenditures of the country's households are for staples. Many households and individuals, however, have a surplus left after they have satisfied their requirements for staple goods. With the advance of prosperity, this surplus grows larger.

The sellers of specialties compete keenly for this surplus. The competition is not only between two similar specialties, such as two different makes of player-pianos but between different kinds of specialties as well; if the surplus is spent for an automobile, consideration of the player-piano will be put off for a year. Because of this double competition and because of the necessity of creating a compelling desire and making a strong close in each individual case, the specialty salesman is of a high type and earns a large remuneration.

20. Specialties become staples. A great many of the staples of today were the specialties of yesterday. Adam Smith says that in 1775 both men and women in England wore shoes; in Scotland, only men wore them;

and in France, neither men nor women wore shoes. In England, then, shoes were a staple commodity; in Scotland, they were staple among men, but a specialty among women; and in France, they were a specialty for both men and women. That is, there existed no demand for them among the women of Scotland, nor among the men or women of France. The people had to be educated to their use; a fairly general desire for shoes had to be created. Even such common articles as toothbrushes, soap, and underclothing have not always been staples, and they are staples today only in the more civilized countries. Their introduction in some foreign parts is only beginning.

There may be those who will maintain that goods are not manufactured prior to a demand for them, but are produced only in response to a very definite demand. Those who have studied the history of selling, however, realize that the demand has to be manufactured just as surely as do the goods. For a long time railroad men laughed at Westinghouse and his air-brakes with which he proposed to stop trains with wind. A Boston mob destroyed the first sewing machine on the ground that it would throw people out of work. It took a long campaign of education to convince people that Edison's electric lights were safe, practical, and better than gas. Only recently has it become the rule to equip newly built houses for electric lighting. The struggle of the telephone for recognition is still fresh in the minds of men of this generation. No business man can now imagine how he could get along without a telephone, but it took real salesmen to convince him in the early days that there was any advantage in them. It is said that one of the first Chicago firms to install telephones subsequently had them removed because the frequent 'phone calls from customers disturbed the clerks.

The same process by which a specialty becomes staple still goes on. In the next few years, we may expect to see the vacuum cleaner just as common as is the sewing machine today. The low-price automobile, too, bids fair to become a staple product. The milestones of civilization are marked by the conversion of specialties into staples through the educating work of salesmen and advertising. The degree of civilization in two countries may be compared by noting to what extent things which have become staples in the one are still specialties in the other.

Points to Ponder

■ Is your product or service a "staple or commodity" or highly specialized? How does that affect your approach to the client?

■ Can you imagine telephones being removed because frequent calls disturbed their clerks?

■ Yes, a cell phone is a staple product today, but there are still differentiators between an Android and an iPhone. Can you name some items that began as specialty items and changed to staples during your lifetime?

■ Do you need to create demand for your product or service? If so, how can you do an even better job driving demand for your solution?

- Do you feel you are best suited for the following and why?

  - ➢ Product sales vs. service sales?
  - ➢ Durable goods vs. Consumer goods?
  - ➢ Larger organizations with many salespeople vs. smaller organizations?
  - ➢ Selling one product vs. multi-line solutions?
  - ➢ Staying in one industry vs. changing over a period of time?

Notes:

LESSON 15 – CLOSING

⌢ ⌣
⌣ **Charlie's Commentary**

Much is written about the art of closing a sale; however, very little is written in our 1914 reference book on this essential sales topic. Closing techniques of the 1950s to the 1980s were amplified by the likes of Tom Hopkins, Brian Tracy, and Zig Ziglar, among others. My first exposure to this was a 1953 classic book by Frank Bettger called *How I Raised Myself from Failure to Success in Sales.* In the book's Foreword, the famous Dale Carnegie praised Bettger and touted how this book is among the best books written on the topic. He goes on to say that he would be willing to walk from New York to Chicago if that is where he needed to go to get it! Quite a recommendation, don't you think? If you enjoy reading about sales from a historical perspective, it is as applicable today as it was over 70 years ago.

As I shared earlier, the classic sales movie *Glengarry Glen Ross* profiles several salesmen working for a less-than-reputable real estate developer. If you think about selling a piece of swamp land to multiple people who would not likely ever go looking at the property, at least not until the sales office was moved to a different city and the salesmen were long gone, you'd be on the right track in understanding the premise of this movie. There is an infamous scene in the movie where the motivational sales manager, played by Alec Baldwin, teaches the A-B-C method. A-Always B-Be C-Closing. Always Be Closing!

Securing a decision is often emotional and generally culminates when the prospective client sees the product or service's value for themselves and is ready to transfer their money in exchange for the value of the goods or services. It does your offering a disservice if you are unable to help the client see its value at the right time. It is also very costly to the salesperson, the company (house), and the client who doesn't benefit from the solution soon enough or, worse, benefits from it through one of your competitors.

In 2003, the company I had recently joined, Integrity Technology Solutions, began data integration projects on behalf of schools. This was a wide-open market at the time, using a technology called the Schools Interoperability Framework (SIF). With only a single client, we went looking for clients across Illinois to have foundational references to sell more schools; after all, who does business with a company with only one client, right?

From 2003 to 2009, our company had grown its reputation for quality solutions and customer service across several states and some very large school systems. We delivered on the promises made, and our clients knew that. By this time, our first client had an even more enormous appetite for data analysis but could not find an out-of-the-box solution that fit them. Besides that, all of the solutions available had very high implementation and ongoing maintenance costs. The school district superintendent was originally not open to a custom solution, but he had grown a significantly high trust level with both me and the delivery of our solutions. The sales closing for what became over $1 million went something like this in the lobby of a conference hotel.

Dave: Bob, I know that you came to this conference looking for the best possible solution for your staff, students, and the district as a whole. What have you found?

Bob: The solutions available continue to impress me. However, they just aren't the right fit. We want to slice and dice the data in ways these companies don't understand. The prices they want for canned software are outrageous, and I can't justify to my board spending money on something that is, in my mind, inferior to what we really need.

Dave: Thank you for being candid with me. As you know, we have discussed creating a custom solution on your behalf before but never explored the cost of doing so. If we could create exactly what you were looking for and could do it for less than any of the proposals you have in hand already, would you be willing to give us the business?

I've shared this story in longer form over the years, but the sales closing conversation was really that simple. To that point, we continued to provide his schools and staff with the highest level of service imaginable. He KNEW us, LIKED us, and most of all TRUSTED us. It would be months before we had completed the requirements gathering, finalize the conceptual designs, and confirm we could meet their cost expectations. Despite the challenges, it remains one of the most rewarding projects I've been part of in my forty-year career.

Finally, there is a book called *Never Be Closing* by Tim Hurson & Tim Dunne, which I've recommended many times over the years. Coincidentally, written in 2014, one hundred years after the words below were penned, the concepts contained in *Never Be Closing* take longstanding concepts about sales and turn them on their head. They lean toward the language associated with section 77 below. Helping the client make a decision that is in their best interest suggests that the client benefits as much or more than the "house" when they decide to sign on the dotted line.

---

76. The close. We now come to the crux of the whole sale—in fact, the crux of all salesmanship. It is the point, too, at which most of our failures become apparent, at least to ourselves. We may sit at the close of each day and plan the work for the next; we may burn the midnight oil studying our goods; we may rack our brains in an effort to clothe uninterested details with a garment of imaginative appeal; we may spend eight hours a day painting beautiful word pictures to numerous prospects; but our work will be largely wasted, or at least will not bring us the results it should, if the selling talk does not have a courageous, compelling close.

If attention has been developed into interest, and if interest has given place to desire, the time to close— that oft-mentioned psychological moment—has arrived. For this psychological moment marks the maximum force of the buying impulse—all inhibiting thoughts have been subjugated and desire is then at its crest. Its presence is sensed by some more readily than others, and sensed by all more easily in some cases than in others. Some profess to know in every case just when it arrives, but to do this would require reading the human mind as an open book and never making a mistake in closing, and no salesman closes all the sales he endeavors to close.

When we say that the psychological moment has passed, we mean that there has been in the sale a time when all inhibiting thoughts were removed, desire created and the man made ready for closing, but that by clumsy closing tactics, an awkward delay, or by talking beyond the point, the prospect has been given an opportunity to create a new set of inhibitions. As one writer has put it, he has recovered his shield of doubt and sword of disagreement and put the salesman to rout.

77. Securing decision. Whether the psychological moment has been sensed, or, on the other hand, the salesman merely feels that he may have created desire, there are certain closing tactics to be gone through. These consist largely of what may be termed the mechanics of closing; and these mechanics are based on the law of positive suggestion.

In this connection it might be well to remind the reader once again that at no point does this text book view the prospect as a victim to be played upon by the salesman against his better interests. And we are not abandoning that attitude now. It is a peculiar fact that nearly all men, except perhaps the biggest of business executives, are cursed, to some extent at least, with indecision and procrastination. They gather all the essential points on some proposition, weigh them pro and con—and then put the whole thing over until the morrow. They want to "think it over." There is a constant danger of over-selling certain merchants, and the salesman should scrupulously avoid this. There are more merchants, however, who do not see or take advantage of their merchandising opportunities and who greatly under-buy. Because the salesman's time is valuable, and because the prospect will never see the advantages of the proposition more clearly than when the whole proposition is fresh in his mind and the salesman is with him, the man who has been convinced must be forced to act—and to act at once.

Except in extremely rare and isolated cases, the salesman need not fear that his closing tactics, no matter how strong or clever they may be, will land an order if his prospect is not convinced—will persuade a man to sign who has not been carried through the other stages, including desire. The real point is that many who have been carried through these previous stages slip away. They desire to "think it over." Even the strongest salesmen do not close every sale where they have brought the prospect to the point of desire. A prospect carried thus far is a distinct asset and the salesman should endeavor to close him.

Points to Ponder

- The following statement is made in section 76, "No salesman closes all the sales he endeavors to close." Is this true today, and if so, why hasn't it changed in over 100 years since it was first written?

- So much is discussed regarding closing, but there is evidence, as presented above, that there are stages in the buyer's mind before the close. What are they, and can you give examples of how this plays out in your business and with your prospective clients?

- Is a salesperson who closes more business more valuable than one who does not? Why do you feel that way?

- Think of a time (or multiple times) when you made a buying decision because the salesperson helped you see that it was in your best interest. Recount the details and ask yourself, "Did you feel manipulated or coerced into a decision?" Think about the title "professional salesperson" and how that would apply to these and other salespeople you know.

Notes:

WHERE DO WE GO FROM HERE?

☺ **Charlie's Commentary**

I started my career in sales in 1984, but quickly landed leadership roles due to the hard work I put into each position I held. I placed great importance on learning all aspects of our business and learning from the best. If you work for an uninspiring leader, two likely scenarios will occur. The first includes following that leader down the path of mediocrity and accepting low-level goals. We'll call this process settling. People settle for second best (or further down the chart) because they don't know better. The second path includes recognizing the leader's inability to lead, and you will walk away from the company and the leader. The longer you are in a role like this, the harder it is to leave (loyalty sets in), and oftentimes, the younger professional doesn't understand their worth in the marketplace, making it more challenging to find that next role.

Sales can be the best profession in the world, but you have to work at it AND enjoy it. If you are unwilling to do both, you might as well look for another profession. I'm not advocating cutting bait sooner rather than later because oftentimes, you can learn from that challenging situation, but in the long run, if you aren't happy, you're not likely to become so.

The path to sales management roles often comes from changing industries or, at the very least, changing companies within the industry you serve. This happens not because the owner doesn't recognize the individual's worth, but most of the time because there is no path for succession. There is only one sales manager, and they will be in that role for another 10-20 years. If you are lucky enough to start in a company of the right size, promotion from within generally pits the person with an inside track against an industry professional with more years of experience, a book of sales they're bringing with them, or a relationship that is key to the new role. Career paths are most often navigated with a mentor's help, especially in the first ten years of one's sales career.

My experience confirms what is shared in #14 below, which suggests that lifelong learners have a distinct advantage over those who are unwilling to learn along the way. Because sales training courses limit the amount of practical experience, nothing beats the college of hard knocks—at least, that's true in the sales profession.

---

11. What the salesman learns. Hugh Chalmers, who has been known as one of America's foremost salesmen, says that a man should always view his compensation from two angles. First, what can he earn? Second, what can he learn? From the latter point of view, salesmanship is especially attractive. The salesman comes into contact with a wide circle of businessmen. He acquires the ability to meet men and to address them. He gets a first-hand knowledge of the big business problem of distribution. He learns to observe the business methods of others. He develops poise and self-confidence and in short acquires the strong, positive qualities that make for success in business.

A great many big business executives began as salesmen. A personal knowledge of conditions on the firing line is invaluable to the man who is directing operations from a private office. The salesman, therefore, who takes advantage of every opportunity for becoming a broad-gauged businessman, and avoids injurious habits, is preparing himself for an executive position, either in the house for which he is selling or in a business of his own building. John North Willys came in from the road where he had been selling automobiles for another concern to establish the Willys-Overland Company of which he is the head today.

With all its opportunities, selling, as a great sales manager has put it, is the most fascinating game in the world; and, unlike most others, is a game of brain, pure and simple. It satisfies the inherent love of adventure— the hazard of defeat and the chance of big victory. To sum up, the man who can sell is a success—others may be.

14. Knowledge plus practice. The trained engineer, fresh from his technical school, is probably not so good a bridge builder as the foreman who has worked at bridge building since he was a boy. Give the engineer five years' experience, however, and he will be the better bridge builder of the two, simply because he has at his disposal, not only his own experience, but the whole past experience of the engineering profession. The salesman, too, needs constant practice. He needs his own experience to tie to the experience of others. But the mediocre man can be improved by teaching; the good man can be made better by teaching; and the best of men can be considerably strengthened by teaching. The great salesman who is born and not made is greater at forty than he was at twenty. A study of the principles of salesmanship will shorten that time between twenty and forty and bring the ambitious man more quickly to his goal.

Points to Ponder

- Regardless of age, do you consider yourself a novice, a developing, or a seasoned sales professional?

- What have you found valuable in gaining the experience & knowledge necessary to become a better salesperson?

- Do you identify with the brief story of John North Willys and see yourself in a leadership role? Is that in a sales manager's role or leading a company at the C-level?

- What one thing can you do today to further your career and professionalism in sales?

SALES MANAGEMENT LESSONS

"Here's your sample case; there's your territory; get the orders."

LESSON 16 - REFERENCES AND LINKEDIN

```
⌐ ˛⌐
  ‿    Charlie's Commentary
```

Why is this the first topic in the Sales Management section? It is simply a reminder that the entire book is over 500 pages, and the Sales Management section itself is nearly 200 pages. The selections that were made were purely subjective on my part to hold your attention. Great details and many lessons are provided in those additional topics.

Therefore, I will only scratch the surface on this topic because so much has been written in blog posts, articles, and paid LinkedIn training that an entire chapter could be devoted to the importance of just this tool. As stated below, references from prospective team members are crucial to making an effective hiring decision. The availability of one's background is so readily available in a LinkedIn profile and a simple Google search that a background check to confirm employment becomes secondary for sales and sales leadership roles.

All that said, what matters is being diligent enough to look closely at the salesperson's LinkedIn page, what others are saying about the candidate, and how they are speaking about others. Have they given others kudos for work that they've done? Have they built two-way relationships? If you haven't done so, be sure to connect with and reach out personally to confirm what has been said online, and you'll likely find the answers you were looking for.

Finally, back in the day, the technology didn't exist (or was just beginning to come along) to confirm what an applicant might provide in a reference. Today, you could pick up the phone, send an email, or verify through the provided LinkedIn messaging. Back then, you had to read between the lines, so to speak, in the letter as is suggested.

---

186. References Just as soon as the formal application has been turned in, the references given by the salesman should be written to. There is a great diversity of opinion as to the value of commendatory letters from those to whom the applicant refers the sales manager. It is contended that there are but few people who will give any but a favorable reference in such a case. It is true that most references will not contain a bald statement of any bad qualities that the applicant may possess. They will be for the most part good, but there are different degrees of good. The sales manager will have no trouble in distinguishing between the genial letter which condemns by faint praise and the sincerely enthusiastic letter that indicates a good opinion. Furthermore, the character of the references given will do something toward showing the applicant's standing or lack of standing in his community.

LESSON 17 - COMPENSATION PLANS

In reading through the following five sections of material, please consider compensation plans you've experienced during your lifetime. Do you lean toward one or another for yourself, and how is that different from what you felt at earlier stages of your life?

I always felt most comfortable with a salary plus commission model for both myself and my teams. Most of the teams I led early in my career were, like myself, younger family men who needed the stability of a salary and the incentive of a commission above a specified level. As described below, this method isn't better or worse than other plans; it has its benefits and drawbacks.

In working with commission-only situations, I found two wonderful success stories worth sharing. The first has to do with the risk associated with betting on oneself. If a salesperson is willing to bet on themselves and accepts a straight commission plan, to begin with a company, I have seen significant self-confidence in them and a propensity to succeed. Once proven to the company (house) many other compensation options open themselves up to the situation. The company has much to gain from retaining these quality salespeople, and investment in them is a key component.

A second commission-only experience that I've encountered mirrors the outlined copy below almost verbatim. In the printing businesses that I owned, ran, and serviced, the cost of goods was known to the salesperson in most instances. If it was in a manufacturing environment, there were "estimating systems" in place, and the salesperson would be positioned to sell at "what the market would bear." In a brokered situation, multiple quotes prove the exact cost of a project so that the salesperson can put on a natural margin or be able to negotiate accordingly.

This practice maximized the profit to the company, the compensation to the salesperson, and, if treated correctly, provided the client with a suitable price model. In many cases, it allowed the salesperson to meet or beat the competitor's price to get in the door, which in turn allowed quality and service to be evaluated by the client. Familiar as it was, we looked for ways to ask the client a basic question: "There are three things available to you: price, quality, and service...which two would you like?"

---

243. What a plan of compensation should accomplish. The objects to be considered in fixing the amount of compensation and the manner in which it shall be paid are: securing the type of men desired; keeping them working at maximum efficiency; and retaining them in the organization. In this connection, it should be remembered that in the beginning of most concerns a strong type of specialty salesman is needed and only that type will succeed. Such men require and are entitled to fairly large incomes. As the proposition becomes better known and better advertised it gradually becomes easier to sell, and then a slightly different type of salesmen may reasonably be expected to succeed. With training methods fairly well established, younger men and men without previous selling experience may be added to the organization. It is not necessary to provide large remuneration for these men at the start. The average cost of making a sale, therefore, can be reduced. This should not be understood to mean that an effort should be made to reduce the incomes of those men who have sold the proposition in its earlier stages. The progress of a salesman who has made good should always be in the other direction. It applies only to new men being added to the organization.

244. Salary and expenses. Salary and expenses is the oldest and probably the most prevalent method of paying salesmen. It affords the sales manager almost perfect control over his men. They can be routed from town to town, instructed how long to stay in a town and whom to see while there. They can be required to make out any reports that the sales manager may deem necessary and be instructed to do no other than selling if emergency requires it. If the house deems it advisable to make small, isolated towns where the sales will be few, and is willing to pay the salesman's salary for doing so, that is the business of the house and not the salesman. The same thing applies to the doing of missionary work where no immediate sales are probable. A firm advertising nationally to create a consumers' demand, and therefore desiring almost perfect distribution will do well to use the salary and expense basis of remuneration.

It has, however, at least one great disadvantage. There is no immediate incentive to strive unceasingly after big business. Of course, the salesman's salary is usually fixed by adding his salary and expenses and determining what percentage of his gross sales they constitute, and raises are made on this basis at the end of the year. This would seem to have the effect of stimulating the men to greater effort but most sales managers would testify that it rather has the effect of causing the salesman to slow down when he is producing sufficient business to warrant his present salary. This is probably further accentuated by reason of the fact that most houses seem averse to allowing a salesman's salary to reach too large a figure, even though the volume of his sales would seem to warrant it.

245. Salary and commission. To combine the advantage of control and direction of the man afforded by the salary basis and the advantage of supplying an incentive to big sales which is inherent in the straight commission plan, many houses base their compensation on a combination of salary and commission. The salary is, of course, smaller than if it were the only remuneration and the rate of commission must be about half or even less than half of that which could be allowed on the straight commission plan. Under this plan the salesman's expenses may or may not be paid by the house. Some houses, in order to strengthen their control over the man, agree to pay his railroad expenses while traveling at the direction of the house.

There are almost countless varieties of the salary and commission plans of payment. Quite a usual provision is to pay no commission in addition to the salary if the salesman takes less than a prescribed amount of business in any period. For an amount of business above his minimum and up to a certain higher amount, a small rate of commission will be paid. Beyond this, the rate of commission gradually increases for increasing amounts of business. In lines where the salesman is allowed leeway in quoting prices, he may be supplied with the cost of each article and his commission figured as a certain percentage of the price he secures over and above this cost figure. This is, of course, a strong incentive to the salesman to hold up prices.

As a general rule it will be found that seasoned salesmen, particularly in specialty lines, will prefer to work on a straight commission basis. The promising young fellow who has never done any selling, however, is loath to try his hand on a straight commission basis even after a thorough training. The salary and commission basis has the advantage over the straight commission plan of attracting this class of new material to the organization.

Increases in the salesman's compensation under this plan may be made either by increasing his salary and allowing his rates of commission to remain stationary, or by allowing the salary to remain stationary and increasing the rates of commission. The former will be found the most feasible method to adopt in case the house has a varied line and a wide range of commission rates on individual items.

246. Straight commission. It is often argued that the house knows what percentage of sales it can afford to pay out in selling expenses and that it will try to avoid paying more than that figure. In its effort to do so, it often pays considerably less and in the last analysis the salesman's compensation will always be fixed on a percentage of sales basis. Why not then pay this percentage out as commission in the first place? It furnishes the salesman with a direct incentive inasmuch as the result of a week's good work is shown immediately in the size of the salesman's weekly remittance. It virtually makes the salesman a partner of the house, the salesman investing his energy and expenses against the house's capital. Doubling his energy, doubles the salesman's earnings. Increases in compensation are taken care of automatically. The house, too, has the advantage of knowing definitely just what its selling expense is going to be. It pays out nothing to the salesman unless orders are actually received.

This plan, too, has its disadvantages. The control of the house over the salesman is weakened. He feels that he is paid a commission for getting business and does not feel under obligation to make out reports. Even if he allows the house to direct his movements within his territory, he will be sure to blame lack of business upon such direction. Usually he will insist that as his earnings are dependent upon his good judgment, he should be allowed to assume full direction of his own work. It is doubtful if it is ever possible to direct the salesman to the same extent as under a salary arrangement.

There is danger, furthermore, of the salesman's feeling that he is under no obligation to work constantly; his money stops when he stops, so whether he works or not is entirely his own affair. It has previously been pointed out that this attitude is likely to cause fluctuations in the amount of business and variations in the expense of handling it at the house. The chances are that territory will not be worked as thoroughly as the sales manager would like to have it worked. In some lines, the commission salesman may more readily oversell a dealer than would the salesman on a salary. It should be mentioned here that loyalty and a proper esprit de corps in the organization will eliminate, to some extent at least, certain of the disadvantages enumerated.

247. The drawing account. Some houses allow a drawing account in connection with the straight commission plan of compensation. A salesman starting in and having a family to support or other obligations to meet is likely to desire a drawing account to guard against any unexpected delay in reaching a satisfactory volume of sales. Another may wish to equalize his income by taking a stipulated amount each week in place of widely varying commission checks. And it must be confessed that some salesmen expect to be in debt to their concerns constantly.

There was a time when drawing accounts were pretty freely granted and it was not unusual for an unscrupulous individual to be receiving drawing accounts from several different sources. Most houses today, where a drawing account is allowed, insist upon its being regarded strictly as money borrowed which must be repaid at the first opportunity. Overdrafts are held down not only because the sales manager does not wish to place himself in a position where the salesman's leaving will cause a heavy loss to the concern—for overdrafts which are paid up after the salesman leaves are the exception—but because overdrafts represent a reduction of the concern's cash resources.

In a few exceptional cases a drawing account will be guaranteed. That is, a certain amount of money will be paid to salesmen periodically for a stipulated time, and will be deducted from the salesman's earned commissions; but he will be under no obligation to pay back any money in case his commissions fall short of the guaranteed amount. In general, it may be said that the practice of allowing drawing accounts is being much curtailed.

LESSON 18 - TERRITORY SIZE

☺ **Charlie's Commentary**

Our world today has grown much larger than it was in 1914. With internet technology, video and phone conferencing, coupled with global manufacturing and shipping, business can be done all over the world. Industrial trade existed 100 years ago; however, with consumer goods and raw materials, doing so was severely hampered by transportation.

Focusing domestically, the United States' westward expansion had occurred by 1914, and the last two contiguous states joined the union in 1912, New Mexico and Arizona. However, without an interstate system to transport by freight truck was undeveloped, and the first airmail service didn't exist. The first airmail flight took place in 1918.

Selling in the larger cities was far easier than traveling to rural areas. Products produced in one area of the country (say, furniture in North Carolina) were conveniently shipped by rail to places with rail service. The salesperson who serviced specific geographic regions was bound to see as many as they could in their particular market. However, as businesses and consumers sprawled out, it became ever more challenging for the companies to keep up with small sales teams. The sales profession was evolving, and the rules around commission, territory, and all other aspects were up for negotiation.

When I began my sales career in 1984, territory size was a hot topic. If you have ever had your sales territory "squeezed" by a company, you understand precisely what I mean. Companies (particularly in the printing industry) were interested in gaining as much business as possible, and capturing house accounts that were now outside the new salesperson's territory was commonplace.

In the companies I've managed, I have never worried about the size of a territory nor shared the challenges that have existed with others. I have always felt that the market was large enough (even in a single city) that my sales team could find another client. As far as I was concerned, if my salesperson needed to look over their shoulder and wonder where their counterparts were, they would have far too much time on their hands.

248. Blocking out territory. Territory is a distinct asset to the house. The sales manager should have a clear idea of the value of this asset and the returns to be expected from it. A territory that is too small will discourage the salesman and prevent his producing a large volume of sales. A territory which is too large will be skimmed; and the house, therefore, will not get all the business to which it is entitled. In the early stages of a proposition, the territory seems large and the number of salesmen available small. The house can be liberal with territory. Eventually there comes a time, however, when territory must be worked intensively if the house is to continue to grow. If, when the house has covered as large an area in search of business as the nature of its products will permit, territories are twice as large as they should be, the house will be doing but half the business that would be possible if territories were divided and the force of salesmen doubled.

Figures showing territorial conditions may come from the United States Census, governmental reports and trade journals; previous experience and records of the firm's personal investigations made by the sales manager, his assistants or field representatives; and from listing and directory concerns whose business it is to compile this sort of information.

The sales manager will know what classes of people or businesses are possible prospects. From one of the sources enumerated, the number of prospects in the area to be covered should be ascertained by subdivisions. For example, if the whole United States is to be covered the number of prospects by counties may be the basis of apportioning territories. In the case of a jobbing house serving a more limited area, the number of prospects in each town can be tabulated. Next, the number of prospects that a salesman can call upon and dispose of daily should be determined. Then it should be decided how often a territory must be thoroughly worked. The wholesale grocery house will have its salesman call upon its customers every two weeks. The dry-goods salesman will probably call about four times during the year. In the case of some specialties where a man is sold but once, it may be well to allow a considerable lapse of time between workings of a particular town or county. With the information indicated in hand, it will be possible in most lines, by multiplying the number of prospects that can be seen in a day by the number of days that should elapse between workings of a territory, to estimate the number of prospects that should be contained in the ideal territory.

Each territory should then be laid out as nearly as possible with a view to making all parts easily accessible from some central starting point. This will diminish the amount of railroad fares and enable the salesman to get to his headquarters more frequently. This is especially important when the salesman has a family. It will be seen that territories in the East will be fairly compact while those in sparsely settled districts in the West may cover a considerable area and necessitate much traveling. This will tend to cut down the number of prospects in an ideal territory in the West and increase the number in eastern territories.

249. Apportioning city territory. In handling a product, prospects for which are fairly numerous, it will often be found necessary to have more than one salesman stationed in large cities. The city may then be district-ed or it may be found advantageous to apportion certain classes of prospects to each salesman irrespective of the prospect's location in the city.

Notes:

LESSON 19 - GETTING THE BEST OUT OF THE SALES TEAM

ʕ•ᴥ•ʔ **Charlie's Commentary**

Some interesting nuggets of information are contained in these final sections, especially if you've been in a sales leadership role for any length of time or if you've had significant interactions with a truly respected sales manager. I was promoted to national sales manager in 1986, just two years after joining Professional Business Systems right out of college. I had sold encyclopedias and educational materials that went along with them, my first summer after graduation, and found that one-call closes selling Grolier Encyclopedias was not my destiny after a poor experience with their sales manager. I won't go into great detail, but that sales manager did not follow many of the tactics contained in these pages and, at one point, told me that I could not succeed in the long term but that I was just getting "lucky." It wasn't said in a revering way either.

In 1986, with little to no sales leadership training, I began hiring salespeople who were young and ambitious like myself. Initially, in addition to managing the others, I serviced a territory of my own. This not only kept me in front of the client, but it also gave me sound judgment when the other salespeople had excuses. My tolerance for inactivity, lack of interest, and focus was very short. My concern was helping the salesperson reach profitability soon. In the process, I was not always building relationships within my team. Later, I would find that the tact with which I reprimanded cost precious time and resources, leaving salespeople in my wake.

If we contrast this with the words contained in sections 263-265, the success of the sales professional appears to hinge on encouragement, and those methods were Neanderthal-like in 1914 due to the restrictions of travel, technology, and communication. Today, we can text words of encouragement, send emails, or phone the salesperson's cell. We can provide or create incentives by offering benefits that may not have been there before (gym memberships, coffee cards, health insurance, expense reimbursements, mileage, etc.), and the company can provide behind-the-scenes marketing that provides countless leads. Remember when your parents said, "Back in the day, we had to walk uphill both ways to school and do it in a blizzard without shoes..."? My interpretation of a sales talk might sound like this: "Back in my day, I didn't have a CRM system and had to rely on seeing parked cars in a parking lot to see how busy a prospect's office might be. We didn't have the internet to look up names, we actually had to walk into the business and ask who took care of the ordering of X, Y, or Z. And if the receptionist had been trained to send you packing before you got the first sentence of your elevator talk out of your mouth, I knew there was no chance of seeing that client anytime soon. So shut up and get back to work!"

---

261. The biggest thing in sales management— Here is the sales manager's real task, the end of all sales management—getting the best out of the men in the field. Some sales managers claim that this is the only thing they should be called upon to do, and some houses insist that the energies of their sales managers be directed to this end to the exclusion of all other duties. With the proviso that in order to accomplish this objective the sales manager must be a broad-gauge, all-round business man and that his authority and activities should have the wide scope indicated in previous chapters, this is sound doctrine. The sales manager should be careful to delegate to others all routine work and as much detail as is practicable, so that he shall have ample time, thought, and energy to devote to his most important object of getting the best out of every individual member of his organization.

262. "Ginger" versus cooperation. —A sales manager once sent out to each of his men a letter reading in part as follows: "Why did you fall down in making the sale? For your own benefit and ours, write me frankly." He was rather startled to receive from one of his men this reply: "Because I did not know my goods. You have been filling us so full of 'ginger' and 'boost' that we have not had a chance to learn anything about the goods."

There would seem to be two distinct classes of sales managers, one with the pure "ginger" idea of stirring the men up and getting the most from them; and the other with the idea of really giving the men an opportunity to know their goods, of helping them over the rough spots, and of giving them real assistance in the upbuilding of their characters and capacities and the realizing of their ambitions.

Salesmen do not take as kindly to being "gingered" continually as some sales managers fondly imagine. It is true that salesmen, as well as all other men, like a game and take kindly to the introduction of the game spirit into their work, but it must be realized that they are capable, intelligent and ambitious men. They demand that much of common sense be mixed with the game if it is to be successful. From the sales manager's point of view, pure "ginger" methods are inefficient because the enthusiasm they generate is not lasting. The "ginger" idea has a place in sales management only when it has for its foundation a profound love for the men of the organization, a keen realization of their problems and difficulties, and a sincere desire to give them real cooperation.

With these considerations in mind, let us consider the various tested methods of getting the best from the members of the selling organization.

263. Visiting the men in the field. —When the salesmen get into the house but once or twice a year, or have headquarters in their territories and see the home office only at convention time, the sales manager will do well to arrange one or two trips annually during which he will visit and possibly work with each member of his organization. Those whom he may be unable to see should be visited by his principal assistant. When the sales manager and his assistant can each make two trips a year, those visited by the assistant on the first trip should be visited by the sales manager on the second, and vice versa. There is nothing that will put the sales manager closer to his men, and secure a greater measure of their loyalty and enthusiastic support, than to sit down with them in their own headquarters, discuss territory conditions, and get acquainted with their wives and families.

In the case of a general sales manager having control of a number of district offices, this will have to be confined to visits to the district managers, but the district manager should, in turn, keep in touch with the individual men. A variation of this is the calling of individual men into the home office for conferences regarding their work and conditions in their territories.

264. Daily letters. —The average salesman is sensitive, highly strung, and temperamental. If he were not, he would be but an indifferent salesman. Each rebuff, each discouragement, each discourtesy to a man of this nature is likely to take just a little of the edge from his enthusiasm. This enthusiasm must be renewed from some source and, with few exceptions, salesmen will not find the source within themselves. The only source then is contact with the men from the home office. For that reason, the sales manager, or in the case of a large force his principal assistant, should write every day to each individual member of the organization a stimulating, friendly letter. So important are such letters that nothing should be allowed to stand in the way of getting them out. If necessary, a hard and fast rule should be made that all dictation of this nature be in the mails before the sales department force goes home. It may even be well to schedule the mailing so that the letter reaches the salesman at the time when it will be most effective—in the morning just before he goes forth to meet his first prospect. Great care should be taken to mail the letter to the proper town; a salesman who is looking forward to an inspiring message from his sales manager will not be one hundred percent efficient if it fails to arrive. Furthermore, two or three letters reaching a man at the same time will not generate the same amount of enthusiasm as will those same letters reaching him on separate days.

In this connection, it should be remembered that a holiday when no letters are written from the home office will cause the salesman to be without his daily letter on a later working day. To take care of this, it may be well to get out a double amount of letters on the day preceding and delegate some member of the office force to mail them on the holiday. In lieu of this, the sales manager may get out a postcard containing some timely message in multigraphed form or send to each man in the organization an ordinary picture postcard on which he has written some personal message. The latter course can profitably be followed too, when the sales manager or his assistant is out on the road. In the latter case, the salesman will receive the personal card in addition to his usual daily letter.

265. Contents of daily letter. —In these letters the salesmen should be thanked sincerely for the orders received from them that day or for contributions to the house organ. They should be complimented upon any good work they may have been doing and should receive sound advice from the sales manager on any deals that may be before them. The message will, in general, be based upon the letter received that morning from the salesman.

All criticism should, in so far as it is possible, be kept out of these letters. If any is absolutely necessary, it should be given in a manner calculated to increase rather than decrease the salesman's efficiency. A salesman who has been doing his best, but for some reason has not been producing normal results, needs friendly encouragement and sound suggestions rather than criticism. Nothing will so effectively destroy the producing power of a loyal salesman as a sharp, fault-finding letter from the sales manager. If the salesman has been derelict and it is necessary for the sake of discipline that he be reprimanded, the language in which the reprimand is couched should be given careful consideration. There is no phase of the sales manager's duty in which he is called upon to exercise more tact and real executive ability than in his letters to his men. His one purpose is to increase sales, and in every letter he should have in mind the ultimate effect upon the productiveness of the salesman.

Points to Ponder:

- If you are in a sales leadership role, would you prefer to have the tools available today or those from 1914? Why or why not? Can you imagine writing a letter a day and shipping it to them in the field?

- Professional development and mentorship are crucial for sales leaders, especially younger salespersons. Where can you find proper training or examples of excellent sales leadership?

- Are you open to evaluating how you motivate your team and compensate them accordingly? Are things so different today than they were in the past?

- Given your time in a sales leadership role, what has changed even in that time?

Notes:

Recommended Reading

Harry Truman famously said, "Not all readers become leaders, but all leaders must be readers."

Truman's study of history proved indispensable. According to Truman Library Supervisory Archivist Samuel Rushay, "It provided him ethical and moral guidance and was a tool that he used to make decisions, most notably as President of the United States during his two terms of office....Truman 'internalized' history and looked to the past almost reflexively whenever a problem or issue arose."

https://www.trumanlibraryinstitute.org/tru-history/

Whether you are a reader, leader, or both, summers offer the opportunity to delve into one or more of President Truman's most read and often recommended volumes.

- *Plutarch's Lives*
- *Caesar's Commentaries*
- *Benjamin Franklin's Autobiography*
- Gibbons' *Decline and Fall of the Roman Empire*
- *Bunker Bean* by Harry Leon Wilson
- *Missouri's Struggle for Statehood, 1804-1821* by Floyd Calvin Shoemaker
- *Plato's Republic*
- *Complete works* of Robert Burns
- *Complete works* of Lord Byron (George Gordon), especially Childe Harold
- Edward Shepherd Creasy's *Fifteen Decisive Battles of The World: From Marathon to Waterloo*
- Charles Beard's *An Economic Interpretation of the Constitution*
- William Shakespeare, all writings but especially *Hamlet, King Lear, Othello,* and *The Sonnets*

If a summer reading list that includes Plutarch feels a bit daunting, take this encouragement from Mr. Truman: "It has been a lifetime program for me, and if you start out even on this incomplete list, you will find it a lengthy study but well worthwhile. It will keep you out of mischief, too."

Do you think Harry Truman would be proud of you if you read all twelve of the volumes he's mentioned above, or do you think he would applaud your efforts to begin working on the list? His famous quote about readers being leaders has personally led me to pursue a lifelong learning mindset and to talk about Sales and Sales Leadership as a profession. Modern Business from the Alexander Hamilton Institute contains volumes of work on the subjects of sales and marketing in addition to accounting, operations, and business law. However, there are thousands of books on the subject of sales. The following is Charlie's list of recommended sales books; this will get you started, but is certainly not exhaustive.

- *100 Proven Ways to Acquire and Keep Clients for Life* - C. Richard Weylan
- *Blind Broom Salesman* – Barbara Baldwin
- *Driving Demand* – Elizabeth Allen
- *How I Raised Myself Up from Failure to Success* – Frank Bettger
- *How to Master the Art of Selling* – Tom Hopkins
- *Little Red Book of Selling* – Jeffrey Gitomer
- *Never Be Closing* -Tim Hurson and Tim Dunne
- *See You at the Top* – Zig Ziglar
- *Silver Boxes* – Florence Littauer
- *Streetwise to Saleswise* – Jeff West & Bob Burg
- *The Go-Giver* and *The Go-Giver Sells More* – Bob Burg
- *The One Minute Salesperson* – Spencer Johnson
- *The Referral Engine* – John Jantsch

Your Favorite Sales/Business Books

- _____
- _____
- _____
- _____
- _____
- _____

9 7 8 1 5 0 6 9 1 5 0 8 1